upper-intermediate

second edition

w o r k b o o k

Innovations

a course in natural English

Morgan Lewis

THOMSON
™

United Kingdom • United States • Australia • Canada • Mexico • Singapore • Spain

THOMSON

™

Innovations Upper-Intermediate
Workbook
Second Edition
Morgan Lewis

Publisher: *Christopher Wenger*
Series Editor: *Jimmie Hill*
Editorial Manager: *Howard Middle/ HM ELT Services*
Director of Marketing, ESL/ELT: *Amy Mabley*
Developmental Editor: *Paul MacIntyre*
Editorial Assistant: *Lisa Geraghty*
Sr. Production Editor: *Sally Cogliano*
Associate Marketing Manager: *Laura Needham*
Sr. Print Buyer: *Mary Beth Hennebury*

Compositor: *Process ELT (www.process-elt.com)*
Production Management: *Process ELT*
Illustrator: *Peter Standley*
Photography Manager: *Sheri Blaney*
Photo Researcher: *Process ELT*
Copyeditor: *Process ELT*
Cover/Text Designer: *Studio Image & Photographic Art*
(www.studio-image.com)
Printer: *G. Canale & C. S.p.A*

Printed in Italy.
3 4 5 6 7 8 9 10 07 06

For more information contact Thomson Learning, High Holborn House, 50/51 Bedford Row, London WC1R 4LR United Kingdom or Thomson ELT, 25 Thomson Place, Boston, MA 02210 USA. You can visit our Web site at elt.thomson.com

For permission to use material from this text or product contact us:
Tel   1-800-730-2214
Fax   1-800-730-2215
Web   www.thomsonrights.com

ISBN: 0-7593-9850-X
(Workbook)

ISBN: 0-7593-9847-X
(Coursebook)

ISBN: 0-7593-9846-1
(Audio Tapes)

ISBN: 0-7593-9844-5
(Audio CDs)

ISBN: 0-7593-9849-6
(Teacher's Book)

ISBN: 0-7593-9848-8
(Teacher's Resource Book)

Photo Credits

Page 13 © William Fritch/Brand X Pictures;
Page 15 © William Fritch Brand X Pictures;
Page 48 © AP Photo/U.S. Coast Guard Cdr. James Manning, ho;
Page 51 © Digital Vision Ltd;
Page 59 AP Photo/Cesar Rangel;
Page 61 AP Photo/Donna McWilliam;
Page 71 AP Photo/FordMotor Co;
Page 76 © Frank Conway/Index Stock Imagery

All other photos are by Painet Inc.

To the student

Studying on your own outside class is just as important as the work you do with your teacher. Learning is not something which happens immediately or when you want it to happen! Learning is a slow process. You can make the process faster and more efficient if you study at home.

- Do a little every day rather than a lot once a week.
- Try to do an exercise first without using the answer key, but don't be afraid to use the answer key, if you have a problem.
- In some exercises there may be more than one correct answer. This is perfectly normal. There is often more than one way to say something.
- Before you start working on your own, study the exercises on page 7.

Contents

Unit 1
Talking about people 8

1 Present simple
2 Present simple and present continuous
3 Look, sound, smell, feel
4 Expressions with prepositions
5 Phrasal verbs with *with*
6 Keep
7 Expressions with *make* and *do*
8 *Make* and *do* in context
9 Countries, nationalities and languages
10 Describing people
11 Adjectives and modifiers
12 As long as
13 Writing: an article

Unit 2
Friends and relatives 13

1 *Re-* verbs
2 Verb collocations
3 All I want to do is ...
4 Not as ... as ...
5 The more ... , the more ...
6 Crime
7 Writing: a composition

Unit 3
Your interests 16

1 Expressions with *not*
2 Go and ...
3 Frequency expressions
4 So (do) I, Neither (do) I
5 Used to
6 Football and tennis
7 Books and newspapers
8 *Go, play* or *do*?
9 Prepositions
10 Writing: your interests

Unit 4
Unusual interests 20

1 *-ing* forms
2 Paragraph ordering
3 Otherwise
4 More *-ing* forms
5 Need + *-ing*
6 Prepositions
7 Abbreviations
8 Collocations: *decision*
9 Words ending in *-ism*
10 Writing: an article

Unit 5
Big decisions 24

1 Giving explanations: past perfect continuous
2 What's the job?
3 Second conditionals
4 *Wish* and conditionals
5 Famous conditionals
6 Question tags
7 You don't ... , do you?
8 I knew I'd have to ...
9 Stuck
10 It's just as well
11 Encouraging expressions
12 Collocations
13 Why? How come?
14 Writing: a letter

Unit 6
Flying 29

1 Airports and planes
2 Idioms focus
3 Phrasal verbs with *up*
4 Comparatives
5 Absolutely
6 Infinitive or *-ing* form 1
7 Infinitive or *-ing* form 2
8 Quick verb check
9 Expressions with *in*
10 Expressions with *mind*
11 Writing: a formal letter

Unit 7
Your weekend 34

1 Future arrangements
2 Will/won't
3 *Going to* and *'ll*
4 Asking about plans
5 Collocations: *meeting, appointment, date*
6 Reading: future forms
7 Myself
8 Going to have to

Unit 8		1	Try and …	6	Expressions with *give*
Party animals	37	2	Time prepositions: *at, on, in*	7	Time and money
		3	It's a great place	8	Verb + preposition
		4	Verb collocations	9	Writing: a story
		5	Weak, weaken		

Unit 9		1	Collocations: *have, get*	6	*I bet* + auxiliary
Last night	41	2	Had to	7	Until
		3	Managed to	8	So/such
		4	Sleep and dreams	9	Writing: an awful experience
		5	Responding with auxiliaries		

Unit 10		1	He fancies you!	7	Modal verb expressions
Relationships	44	2	Vocabulary: prefixes	8	Won't
		3	Expressions with *break*	9	*Can't have/must have* + past participle
		4	Phrasal verbs with *break*	10	Writing: an e-mail
		5	Expressions with *on* 1		
		6	Expressions with *on* 2		

Unit 11		1	Finish the story	6	Have something done
Telling stories	47	2	Adverbs 1	7	*-ing* clauses
		3	Adverbs 2	8	Train vocabulary
		4	Adverbs 3	9	Storytelling expressions
		5	Shall I … or not?	10	Vocabulary

Unit 12		1	Cash and banks	6	Conjuctions: *while, during, for*
Difficult to believe	51	2	Money expressions	7	*Some* and *any*
		3	I shouldn't have done that	8	Expressions with *take*
		4	Past simple and past continuous	9	Vague language
		5	Pairs of verbs	10	Writing: a naughty incident

Unit 13		1	Past simple and present perfect	5	Ending a conversation
Old friends	55	2	Present perfect simple and present perfect continuous	6	*It's time* + past simple
		3	For/since	7	Still, yet, already
		4	Expressions with *for*	8	I wish

Unit 14		1	Expressing disapproval	6	Adjective + preposition
Art	58	2	Not recommending something	7	*The* or no *the*
		3	Collocations: *cause*	8	Remind, remember
		4	Adding a comment	9	I keep meaning to …
		5	Believe it or not	10	Writing: an article

Unit 15
Describing things 62

1 Taste, smell, feel
2 Opposites
3 Collocations
4 Linked questions
5 Considering, although
6 In spite of
7 ... , though
8 Negative questions
9 Expressions with *way*
10 Easily the biggest
11 Comparison
12 Must've

Unit 16
Films and television 66

1 At the cinema
2 Water metaphors
3 *-ed* adjectives
4 The best film I've ever ...
5 Past perfect
6 Prepositional phrases
7 Typical mistakes
8 Expressions with *out of*
9 Mixed conditionals

Unit 17
Cars and cities 69

1 *If* suggestions
2 Auxiliary verbs
3 Cars
4 Traffic signs
5 Traffic offences
6 The fact that
7 Compound adjectives
8 Make, let
9 The passive
10 Expressions with *all*
11 Agreeing expressions
12 Writing: a balanced composition

Unit 18
Annoying things 74

1 Verb collocations
2 Collocations: *issue*
3 Phrasal verbs
4 Complaining
5 Complaining and apologising
6 Explain, ask
7 Was/were going to
8 Jokes: complaining
9 Collocations: *problem*
10 Writing 1: a letter of complaint
11 Writing 2: a complaint anecdote

Unit 19
Your future 78

1 Starting with *what*
2 I might try and ...
3 Planning structures
4 Sentence adverbs
5 *if* expressions
6 If things ...
7 Just do it!
8 Present perfect for the future
9 Future collocations
10 Collocations
11 Phrasal verbs with *up*

Unit 20
The world of work 82

1 Working conditions
2 Getting a job
3 Collocations: adjective + *job*
4 Collocations: *career*
5 Expressions: *boss* or *employee*?
6 Describing your job
7 Two views of work!
8 Passing on messages
9 Future continuous
10 Reporting verbs
11 Writing: a report

Answer Key 86

Introduction

1 | Words, phrases, expressions

Everyone knows what a *word* is. An *expression* is the general word we use in this course for a phrases – two or more words – which go together in a fixed way. For example:

We had *the time of our lives*.
He's *similar to* his brother.
I'm *not very interested in* sport.

Underline the expressions in each of these sentences.

1. I'm quite interested in gardening.
2. We're up to our eyes in work.
3. Strawberries are very cheap at the moment.
4. The film was too violent for my taste.
5. Let's go. It's getting late.
6. She's very keen on tennis.
7. I think I'm in a rut.
8. I'm feeling a bit off colour.

Which expression meant *ill*? It is important to understand that expressions can be difficult to translate. You can't translate word for word. Instead, you need to find the equivalent expression in your own language.

2 | What is a collocation?

A *collocation* is two or more words which regularly occur together. The collocation exercises in this book bring together collocations which have something in common – for example, collocations with the word *job*. Underline the most useful collocations in these sentences. The first one is done for you.

1. I really don't like <u>strong tea</u>.
2. Did I hear that John is getting married?
3. It was dry wine we asked for, I'm afraid.
4. He's got a very demanding job.
5. I think we're going to make a loss this year.
6. I fell into a very deep sleep.
7. I've just taken up golf.
8. I'm having to cancel my dentist's appointment.
9. Do you mind if I give you a piece of advice?

3 | Phrasal verbs

Phrasal verbs are verbs followed by one or more prepositions. Underline the phrasal verbs in these sentences.

1. How are you getting on with your mother?
2. Sometimes I feel like giving up my job and retiring.
3. Let's go ahead and order.
4. The meeting dragged on for hours.
5. Let's hurry up. We're running out of time.
6. I'll pick you up at the station.

Sometimes, as in the last example, the verb and preposition are separated.

4 | Grammatical terms

Here is a list (a–h) of some common grammatical terms used in this book. Match them to the sentences 1–8.

1. I've been waiting for hours.   a. present simple
2. We got stuck in the traffic.   b. past simple
3. Where have you been?   c. present perfect
4. I don't drink.   d. past perfect
5. I'd never seen anything like it   e. present continuous
   before.   f. past continuous
6. She'd been planning the party   g. present perfect
   for months.   continuous
7. I'm not feeling very well.   h. past perfect
8. We were just thinking of   continuous
   going.

Now match the sentences 9–18 to the terms i–r.

9. might   i. a gerund
10. Don't you work?   j. an infinitive
11. although   k. a question tag
12. Eventually   l. a second conditional
13. I want <u>to see</u> it.   m. a comparative
14. If I heard, I'd ring.   n. a conjunction
15. better than   o. a negative question
16. I love <u>skiing</u>.   p. a compound adjective
17. a <u>two-year-old</u> girl   q. a sentence adverb
18. It's yours, <u>isn't it?</u>   r. a modal verb

1 Talking about people

1 Present simple (CB page 13)

Complete the text below with the correct form of the verbs in the box.

cause	get up	have	put on	start
deal with	go	open	stand	work

Des Little has a regular nine to five job in a flower shop. Nothing very special about that! But on Friday nights, Des closes the shop, (1) . . . . a black bomber jacket and Doc Marten boots and (2) . . . . outside 'Odyssey', the biggest club in town.

Des is a bouncer – or to use the technical term, a door supervisor. He's over six feet tall and is built like a brick wall. Not many people (3) . . . . arguments with Des!

'Occasionally someone (4) . . . . trouble, usually because they've had too much to drink, but we (5) . . . . troublemakers without too much fuss,' says Des. 'Some of the old ladies in the flower shop are more difficult to deal with than drunken clubbers!' The only problem he (6) . . . . is getting up on Saturday morning. 'I (7) . . . . till four in the morning, then (8) . . . . to bed for four hours. I (9) . . . . at eight. The shop (10) . . . . at nine. It's not easy, I can tell you!'

2 Present simple and present continuous (CB page 13)

Choose the correct form.

1. I'm going to be late home this evening. *I work / I'm working* late.
2. Sorry I can't meet you after work. *I work / I'm working* late on Tuesdays.
3. A: *Do you do / Are you doing* anything interesting this weekend?
   B: Yes, I am, actually. *I go / I'm going* riding.
4. A: Would you like a beer?
   B: No thanks, *I drive / I'm driving*.
5. I don't know what's wrong with me. *I don't sleep / I'm not sleeping* well at the moment.

6. I can't drink wine. *It gives / It's giving* me a headache.
7. I love a good novel. On average, *I read / I'm reading* about one a week.
8. Did you know that Venice *sinks / is sinking*? I wouldn't like to live there, would you?
9. A: Are you going to walk into town?
   B: No, *we take / we're taking* a taxi.
10. My eyes *get / are getting* tired if *I work / I'm working* too long on the computer without a break.

3 Look, sound, smell, feel

Complete these sentences with the correct form of *look, sound, smell* or *feel*.

1. A: OK, I'm ready. Let's go.
   B: You can't wear that shirt with those trousers. It . . . . ridiculous.
2. A: Mm, what are you cooking? It . . . . great!
   B: Oh, I'm trying out a new Chinese recipe.
3. A: I've just booked a holiday in the Bahamas.
   B: The Bahamas? That . . . . fantastic.
4. A: I like that jacket in the window. Do you think it's real leather?
   B: Well, it . . . . real. Go inside and ask.
5. A: The train to Paris costs £95 return.
   B: Are you sure? That . . . . expensive to me.
6. A: Mm, you . . . . nice. What is it? Chanel?
   B: No, it's just some cheap perfume, actually.
7. A: This jacket doesn't feel right.
   B: Well, it . . . . all right to me. Very smart!
8. Why didn't you tell me it would be OK to wear jeans? Everyone else is dressed informally. I . . . . very uncomfortable wearing a suit.

Language note

The verbs *look, sound, smell* and *feel* in Exercise 3 are usually used in the present simple. *Look* and *feel* can also be used correctly in the present continuous.

I feel awful.   *You look very well.*
I'm feeling awful.   *You're looking very well.*

If a grammar explanation says that something is usually used in a certain way, it means very often. It does not mean always.

4 Expressions with prepositions

Complete the sentences below with the prepositions in the box.

at	for	from	to	with

1. I'm quite similar .... my brother, I suppose. We're both quite sporty.

2. I'm completely different .... my sister. She's really sociable.

3. My dad is a regional manager. He's responsible .... five shops in his area.

4. After twenty years in the same job, you can understand why I'm a bit bored .... it.

5. My mum's quite fit. She goes running and she's quite good .... tennis as well.

Underline the expressions with the prepositions.

5 Phrasal verbs with *with*

Complete the sentences below with the phrasal verbs in the box.

catch up with	keep in touch with
come up with	put up with
get on with	split up with

1. Mark's a bit depressed. He .... his girlfriend last week.

2. I like my boss. She's really easy to ....

3. If that's the best idea you can .... , we might as well all just give up and go home.

4. I've got four old school friends who I still .... by letter.

5. Some eastern European countries are starting to .... the West economically.

6. The buses here are so unreliable, but what can you do? You just have to .... it, don't you?

Can you translate the phrasal verbs into your language?

a. catch up with ....

b. come up with ....

c. get on with ....

d. keep in touch with ....

e. put up with ....

f. split up with ....

6 Keep

We often use *keep* + *-ing* to talk about annoying habits. Complete the sentences below with the adjectives in the box.

absent-minded	accident-prone	boring	difficult
flippant	irresponsible	rude	vain

1. I keep forgetting where I put my car keys. I'm very ....

2. He keeps talking about the same thing all the time. He's really ....

3. He keeps joking all the time. He's never serious about anything. He's very ....

4. He keeps getting drunk. He's very ....

5. She keeps having accidents. She's very ....

6. Don't worry. Bill keeps ignoring me, too. He's really very .... at times.

7. She keeps looking at herself in the mirror. She's extremely ....

8. She keeps disagreeing with everybody. She's a very .... person.

7 Expressions with *make* and *do*

You *make a mistake* but you *do your homework*. Complete these expressions with *make* or *do*.

1. .... me a favour
2. .... a good impression on your boss
3. .... the housework
4. .... a decision
5. .... yourself at home
6. .... your best
7. .... a fortune
8. .... a noise
9. .... some shopping
10. .... a few changes
11. .... your military service
12. .... a fuss about something
13. .... a profit/a loss
14. .... a Japanese course
15. .... a phone call
16. .... a lot of business
17. .... a suggestion
18. .... your hair
19. .... a start
20. .... progress
21. .... an extra year at university
22. .... odd jobs for a living

8 *Make* and *do* in context

Complete these sentences with an expression from Exercise 7.

1. I'm going to buy a new suit for my interview. I want to make . . . .

2. I need more time to think about it. I can't make . . . . just like that.

3. Learning English isn't easy, but I think I'm making . . . .

4. Can you do . . . .? Can you carry this bag for me?

5. Men have to do two years' . . . . in my country.

6. I'll be back in a minute. I just need to make . . . . to my office.

7. Please stop making so much . . . . I can hardly hear myself think!

8. Does he really do . . . . for a living?

9. I sold my old car and made . . . . of over £400.

10. Can I make . . . .? Why don't we send the parcel by courier? It's much safer.

11. Come in. Make . . . .

12. My wife's stopped working, so we need to make . . . . to our lifestyle.

13. I like the way you've had . . . . done. It really suits you.

14. We have very few contacts in Argentina, but we do . . . . in Brazil.

15. My boyfriend's from Tokyo, so I'm thinking of doing . . . .

16. Right, is everybody here, then? Let's make . . . .

17. You'll only make . . . . on the stock market if you invest a lot over a long period.

18. I've decided to do . . . . at university so I can do some research.

9 Countries, nationalities and languages

Complete the sentences in the box below.

Country	People	Language
1. She's from Australia.	She's	She speaks . . . .
2. She's from France.	She's	She speaks . . . .
3. She's from	She's German.	She speaks . . . .
4. She's from Portugal.	She's	She speaks . . . .
5. She's from	She's Brazilian.	She speaks . . . .
6. She's from Austria.	She's	She speaks . . . .
7. She's from	She's Swedish.	She speaks . . . .
8. She's from	She's	She speaks Polish.
9. She's from	She's Spanish.	She speaks . . . .
10. She's from Mexico.	She's	She speaks . . . .
11. She's from	She's	She speaks Japanese.
12. She's from China.	She's	She speaks . . . .
13. She's from	She's Greek.	She speaks . . . .
14. She's from	She's	She speaks Korean.
15. She's from Thailand.	She's	She speaks . . . .
16. She's from	She's Dutch.	She speaks . . . .
17. She's from	She's	She speaks Danish.
18. She's from Turkey.	She's	She speaks . . . .

10 Describing people (CB page 8)

Complete the sentences below with the adjectives in the box.

bright	generous	sociable
conservative	knowledgeable	unreliable

1. My husband won't eat anything unusual. He's very
. . . . when it comes to food.

2. Andrew is a terrific brother-in-law. He's really
. . . . with both his time and his money.

3. Talk to Jason if you want to know about hi-fi
systems. He buys all the magazines every month.
He's very . . . . about things like that. He's
a bit of a nerd, really!

4. My sister's going to do a PhD next year. She's the
. . . . one in the family!

5. The problem with Harry is he doesn't always do
what he says he's going to do. He's a bit
. . . . , if you know what I mean.

6. My parents have a lot of people round for dinner
and things like that. They're very . . . .

11 Adjectives and modifiers (CB page 9)

**Complete the sentences below with the
adjectives in the box. The adjective you use
should have a similar meaning to another
adjective in the sentence. Notice the way
the modifiers are repeated.**

distant	relaxing
irritating	straightforward
laid-back	tricky
predictable	witty

1. A: Did you have any trouble finding the hotel?

   B: No. It was really easy, really . . . .

2. A: I like Clare. She's such a good laugh.

   B: Yes, she's great, isn't she? She's really funny, really
   . . . .

3. A: What's your new manager like? Is she all right?

   B: Yes, she's great. She's really easy-going, really
   . . . .

4. A: How did your exam go? Was it OK?

   B: Well, Paper 1 was fine, but Paper 2 was quite
   difficult, quite . . . .

5. A: Did you know you're no longer allowed to park in
the town centre between nine and six?

   B: I know. It's so annoying, so . . . . How
   do they expect you to go shopping?

6. A: You have to admit that Arsenal are the best team
in England at the moment.

   B: Well, they're very successful, I'll give you that, but
   they're so boring, so . . . .

7. A: Did you have a nice time in Greece?

   B: It was great. All I did was lie on the beach
   reading. It was so peaceful, so . . . .

8. A: Pete's girlfriend's a bit strange, isn't she?

   B: Yes, I know what you mean. She's a bit cold, a bit
   . . . .

12 As long as (CB page 10)

**In the conversation in the Coursebook, Simon
said: 'We get on all right, as long as you steer
clear of certain topics.' Make sentences by
matching the beginnings 1–6 to the endings a–f.**

1. I'll lend you the money ☐
2. We're going walking in the mountains at the
weekend ☐
3. OK, OK, I'll come clubbing with you ☐
4. You can stay at my place if you like ☐
5. I don't mind you being a bit late ☐
6. I'll be there at six ☐

a. as long as you don't mind dogs – I've got two
Alsatians.

b. as long as you don't expect me to dance!

c. as long as the weather's OK.

d. as long as you ring me to let me know.

e. as long as you pay me back by the end of the week.

f. as long as the train is on time.

13 Writing: an article

Your school has a writing competition twice a year. This is the latest topic:

'The oldest person in my family'

Tell us about the oldest person in your family and something about the kind of life they have had. Use these ideas to organise your article:

- Who is it?
- How old is he/she?
- Health

- Married?
- His/her past
- His/her life now

The writer of the most interesting article wins a CD of their choice!

Sample article

Put the phrases A–D in the correct place in the first part of the article below.

> **A.** because she has led such an interesting life
> **B.** and when she married my grandfather
> **C.** but you wouldn't know it
> **D.** but she never remarried

> The oldest person in my family is my grandmother, Alice. She is now in her mid-eighties, ☐ **1** – she looks a lot younger and she is still very active. In fact, she's got more energy than me sometimes!
>
> Her husband – my grandfather – died before I was born, ☐ **2** . She told me she could never love another man like she did my grandfather, so she's lived on her own for about thirty years.
>
> She's full of interesting facts and stories ☐ **3** . She travelled all over the world in her job as a nurse in the army, ☐ **4** , she spent even more time abroad because he worked for the BBC in various countries over the years.

Now put the phrases E–H in the correct place in the second part of the article below.

> **E.** which she misses terribly
> **F.** she has kept in touch with all of them
> **G.** and still gets the occasional visitor
> **H.** it was a bit like the United Nations at times

> She has friends in just about every country you can think of and, the amazing thing is, ☐ **5** . I remember as a child seeing letters arrive from Australia, Turkey, Peru, Japan and she showed me where all these places were on her world atlas. In a way, she was my first geography teacher! When I stayed with her in the summer, there always seemed to be a steady stream of visitors – people of all nationalities, colours, religions, and languages – ☐ **6** !
>
> My grandmother still lives in the same house, which is packed with good memories for me. She doesn't travel abroad now, ☐ **7** , but she still writes hundreds of letters ☐ **8** from somewhere exotic. And you can be sure that when you visit her, she'll have yet another interesting story to tell.

Now write your own article about the oldest member of your family.

2 Friends and relatives

1 Re- verbs (CB page 14)

In the text, on page 14 of the Coursebook, you read that Charles Bronson was *reunited* with his son. There are many useful verbs with the prefix *re-*. Complete the sentences below with the correct form of the verbs in the box.

readjust	remarry	reread
rearrange	re-open	retrain
rebuild	rephrase	re-use
reconsider	resit	rewrite

1. I'm divorced and I'm quite happy being single. I don't think I'll ever . . . .

2. If you fail your exam, you can . . . . it a week later.

3. So, Wednesday at two o'clock, then. If there's a problem, give me a call and we can . . . . the meeting for a more suitable time.

4. I don't understand you. No, let me . . . . that – I'm not entirely sure I understand what you're trying to tell me.

5. Don't throw those envelopes away. I'll . . . . them.

6. I know you don't want to go to university, but I really think you should . . . .

7. The park is closed for the winter. It . . . . at Easter.

8. I can't read with all that noise. I can't concentrate. I keep having to . . . . the same bit.

9. I've had enough of computers. I'm going to leave and . . . . as a nurse.

10. His wife died about a year ago. He's just starting to . . . . his life.

11. I'm not really happy with my essay, but I haven't got time to . . . . it. I've got to hand it in tomorrow.

12. It's taking me a while to . . . . to living with my parents again after a year of travelling.

Language note

Should you spell these *re-* verbs with a hyphen or not? Some are very common and are never spelled with a hyphen. For example:
reconsider   remarry   rewrite

Sometimes the less common ones are written with a hyphen, and also sometimes where a vowel follows *re-*. For example:
re-apply   re-employ   re-supply

2 Verb collocations

Reread the third paragraph of the text about Charles Bronson on page 14 of the Coursebook. Then complete the paragraph below with the verbs in the box.

became	get in touch with	heard
came	get	split up with
began	have	track down

Twenty-five years ago, he (1) . . . . a father, when his son, Michael, was born. However, he (2) . . . . the boy's mother when he (3) . . . . a prison sentence three years later. Last year, though, an old friend managed to (4) . . . . Bronson's son in Liverpool. The news that his father was the infamous 'most dangerous man in Britain' obviously (5) . . . . as a total shock to the son, who nevertheless decided to (6) . . . . his father. When Bronson first (7) . . . . from Michael, he said, 'I was on a mission of madness, now I'm on a mission of peace. All I want to do now is (8) . . . . home and (9) . . . . a pint with my boy.'

3 All I want to do is ...

Notice the final sentence in Exercise 2: 'All I want to do now is get home and have a pint with my son.' Make sentences by matching the beginnings 1–8 to the endings a–h.

1. At the end of a long day at work, all I want to do is ☐

2. I don't really want to go to university. All I want to do is ☐

3. I don't want to go abroad on holiday this year. In fact, I don't really want to go anywhere. All I want to do is ☐

4. I've had enough of living at home with my parents. All I want to do is ☐

5. Look, I don't want to have another argument. All I want to do is ☐

6. I don't expect to be able to speak perfect English. All I want to do is ☐

7. I don't want to be a millionaire or anything. All I want to do is ☐

8. I just need to do a bit of shopping. I won't be long. All I want to do is ☐

a. spend a week at home, just chilling out.

b. go home, cook something simple, and sit down with a good book.

c. explain what happened.

d. be able to hold a conversation in English with anyone I meet.

e. get a few vegetables.

f. get a place of my own.

g. get a job and start earning some money.

h. earn enough money to buy a Porsche or two.

Real English: *chilling out*

Chill out means relax.
A: What are you up to this weekend?
B: Nothing much. I'm going to chill out with a few friends.

---

4 Not as ... as ... (CB page 16)

Put the words in brackets in the correct order to complete the sentences.

1. A: How old do you reckon Tim is?
   B: Only about thirty. He's . . . .
   (old / not / as / looks / as / he)

2. It's not exactly cheap to fly to New York from London, but it's . . . .
   (much / as / not / was / I / as / expecting)

3. A: I've never been ice-skating, but it looks pretty easy.
   B: It's . . . .
   (as / not / looks / as / easy / it)

4. It only took me an hour to drive to Cambridge.
   It's . . . .
   (thought / not / as / as / far / I)

5. I know I haven't played for a while, but I can't believe I'm so tired after one game of squash. I suppose I've got to face the fact that I'm . . . .
   (young / used / not / as / be / to / as / I)

6. A: How was your lecture this morning? As boring as ever?
   B: Well, ... I managed to stay awake this time.
   (boring / as / last / one / the / not / as)

7. A: You've got Eminem's latest CD, haven't you? Is it any good?
   B: It's all right, but it's . . . .
   (as / good / not / as / thought / I / would / be / it)

8. A: Did you have a good time last night? You went out with Alison, didn't you?
   B: Well, it . . . . She brought her brother along with her.
   (as / I / hoping / wasn't / was / fun / much / as)

5 The more ... , the more ...

Here is a common structure which uses the comparative.

The more you study, the more you know.
The more you know, the more you forget.
The more you forget, the less you know.

Complete the sentences below with the pairs of words in the box.

faster, sooner	older, wiser
longer, less	sooner, better
more, more	sooner, sooner

1. Come on, let's go. The . . . . we leave, the . . . . we'll get there.

2. The . . . . I think about what I said to Gill, the . . . . I think I was wrong.

3. Come on. The . . . . we work, the . . . . we can go home.

4. The . . . . I get, the . . . . I become.

5. The . . . . I finish school, the . . . . I just want to get a job.

6. The . . . . I work here, the . . . . I like the way we're treated.

6 Crime

Complete the sentences below with the words in the box.

arrested	parking ticket	speeding
court	shoplifting	stopped
fined		

I once got a(n) (1) .... for parking on double-yellow lines. Another time, I got (2) .... by the police for not wearing a seatbelt, but they didn't do anything. They just checked my licence and then let me go. They could have fined me £50.

A friend of mine had to go to (3) .... a few years ago because he was caught (4) .... He was doing over sixty in a 30 mph zone and he was (5) .... £300.

The worst thing that's happened to anyone in my family was when my fifteen-year-old brother was (6) .... for (7) .... in a department store in France. He said his friends made him do it.

7 Writing: a composition

The composition at the top of the next column is a reaction to the statement:
'**Prisons don't work.**'

Task 1
Put these sentences in the correct place in the composition.

A. The answer to overcrowding, however, is not to build more prisons but to find ways of persuading offenders to turn their backs on the crime and punishment sub-culture they find themselves in before it's too late.

B. Sadly, this is particularly true of young offenders, who often see older, more experienced criminals as role models.

C. For example, it has been proved that offenders who are made to apologise to their victims in public are less likely to re-offend than those who do not.

Although this statement is an over-generalisation, I believe it is basically true, especially for those involved in petty crime.

The fact is, many people who spend time in prison end up going back there sooner or later. The experience of prison does not deter them from re-offending. Worse than that, those in prison for committing petty crimes often mix with other prisoners who are serving sentences for more serious crimes, and their level of involvement in crime can deepen as a result. [1]

I know this is not a popular view, but more time and money should be spent on helping offenders to see how their behaviour affects others, to take full responsibility for their actions, and to choose a different life for themselves. [2]

Prison, or high security hospitals, are a necessity for some – nobody wants dangerous people walking the streets – but for many offenders, prisons are failing to break the cycle of crime, and it is therefore no surprise that prisons are becoming overcrowded. [3] Prisons are clearly not doing that.

Task 2
Write a composition responding to the following:
'**Capital punishment (the death penalty) is never justified.**'

The language in the box below will help you. Check any words you don't know in your dictionary.

Sentence openers The fact is ... It is obvious to everyone that ... Personally, ... Tragically, ...	although a 'life sentence' does not always mean for life; it may be for twenty-five years, for example.) make a mistake wrongly convict someone
Crime violent crime rape murder manslaughter acts of terrorism	**People** the judge the jury the offender the police the victim's family
Verb + noun expressions find someone guilty sentence someone to death impose the death sentence want/demand justice give someone a life sentence (prison for the rest of the offender's life,	**Other words and expressions** proof guilty/innocent a miscarriage of justice on death row (in prison, waiting for an execution date) an act of self-defence

1 Expressions with *not* (CB page 21)

In the listening activity in the Coursebook, you met the expression: 'Not as often as I used to.' Complete these short dialogues by putting the words in brackets in the correct order.

1. A: How often do you go to the dentist?
   B: Not . . . .
   (should / often / I / as / as)

2. A: Do you get to see your parents much?
   B: Not . . . .
   (I'd / as / to / much / like / as)

3. A: Do you ever work on Saturdays?
   B: Not . . . .
   (I / if / avoid / it / can)

4. A: Do you still play a lot of squash, then?
   B: Not . . . .
   (used / to / as / I / as / much)

5. A: The buses here are hopeless. Do you ever use them?
   B: Not . . . .
   (have / I / to / unless)

6. A: Is there a staff meeting this afternoon?
   B: Not . . . .
   (know / as / as / far / I)

2 Go and ... (CB page 22)

In the conversation in the Coursebook, Helena said: 'We could always go and see a film.' *Go and* + verb is very common in spoken English. Complete the short dialogues with the phrases in the box.

ask him	
call a taxi	get some money
find a table	have a coffee
get a bottle of wine	have a look
get it checked	see the doctor

1. A: I'm getting a bit tired. Do you mind if we have a break?
   B: Not at all. Let's go and . . . .

2. A: Come on. I'm hungry. Let's find a restaurant.
   B: Good idea. I just need to go and . . . .
   . . . .
   A: Oh, don't worry. I'll use my credit card.

3. A: Is there somebody at the door? I think I heard something.
   B: Go and . . . . It's probably just the post.

4. A: Has Frank got his car? Maybe he could give us a lift.
   B: Good idea. I'll go and . . . .

5. A: I fancy a Big Mac. What are you going to have?
   B: I'll get them. You go and . . . .

6. A: What are we taking to Lisa's party tonight? Have we got anything?
   B: Oh no, I forgot. I'll go and . . . .

7. A: I don't think I should drive. I've had two glasses of wine.
   B: You're right. I'll go and . . . .

8. A: Does your car normally make that noise?
   B: No, I need to go and . . . .
   It's getting worse.

9. A: What do you think these spots are on my hands? They came up this morning.
   B: They look horrible. You'd better go and
   . . . .

We also say *come and* + verb. For example:

Come and sit down.
Come and see me.
Come and have a look.
Come round and have a meal.

3 | Frequency expressions (CB page 21)

Complete the short dialogues below with the words in the box.

all	few	not
can	half	three
every	much	whenever

1. A: How often do you buy a newspaper?

   B: Two or . . . . times a week, I suppose.

2. A: How often do you get together with your whole family?

   B: . . . . that often. A couple of times a year, I suppose.

3. A: How often do you go sailing, then?

   B: . . . . other weekend. As long as the weather's OK.

4. A: How often do you go out with friends?

   B: A . . . . evenings a week usually.

5. A: Do you use your phone to text much?

   B: Oh yes, ... the time.

6. A: What time is the next train to London?

   B: Ten fifteen. There's a London train every . . . . an hour.

7. A: Your boyfriend's moved to Manchester, hasn't he?

   B: Yes. It's a long way, but we try to see each other as often as we . . . .

8. A: Do you still go to watch Real Madrid play?

   B: Not as . . . . as I used to, but I still go . . . . I get the chance.

4 | So (do) I, Neither (do) I (CB page 23)

Complete this conversation with one word in each space.

Lydia: These buses are always late, aren't they?

Maria: Yes, and I'm in a hurry.

Lydia: Oh, so (1) . . . . I. Where do you work?

Maria: I haven't actually got a job at the moment.

Lydia: Neither (2) . . . . I. I'm on my way to an interview right now. That's why I wish this bus would hurry up.

Maria: That's funny. I'm going to an interview too. Where's yours?

Lydia: It's a firm called Johnson and Cuthberts.

Maria: But so (3) . . . . mine! We must be going after the same job. What a coincidence!

Lydia: And I'm so tired. I didn't sleep last night worrying about it.

Maria: Neither (4) . . . . I. Have you done this kind of thing before?

Lydia: Yes, I used to work for IBM.

Maria: Did you? So (5) . . . . I! I was in exports.

Lydia: I was in accounts. That's why we never met. You must've known Jason.

Maria: Jason? Everyone knew Jason. I used to go out with him for a while.

Lydia: You're kidding! So (6) . . . . I – but only for a couple of weeks! Maybe we should change the subject!

5 | Used to (CB page 24)

Complete the sentences below with the words in the box.

business	time
clothes	trouble
gym	vegetables
painting	weekend

1. I used to run my own cleaning . . . . I sold it about five years ago.

2. I used to do a lot of . . . . when I was younger.

3. When I was at school, I used to get into . . . . quite a lot.

4. I used to spend every . . . . playing football with my mates.

5. I used to grow my own . . . . in the place where we lived before.

6. I used to spend a lot of . . . . down at the beach before I put on so much weight.

7. I used to make my own . . . . when I was a student.

8. I used to go to a . . . ., but I stopped going because I started to look like a gorilla.

Real English: *mates*

Mates are friends (usually male friends).
I went shopping with a few mates.

Complete these sentences with *usually, used to* or *use to*.

9. I .... take the bus to work. It's cheap and there's a stop just outside my house.

10. I'm sure I've seen you somewhere before. Did you .... work in Marks and Spencer's?

11. When I was at school, we always .... try to leave school early on Friday afternoons.

12. I didn't .... like olives but I just love them now. I can't eat enough of them.

13. When I was in my teens, I .... stay out really late listening to music with my friends.

14. What do you .... do on Saturday afternoons?

15. Did *your* parents .... ask you silly questions about where you'd been and who you'd been with?

16. When I was a student, I .... live in a huge house with about twelve other students.

6 | Football and tennis

A *referee* is in charge of a football match, but an *umpire* is in charge of a tennis match. Look at the nouns below. Write F if the word is usually used to talk about football, T if it used to talk about for tennis, or B if it is used for both.

Nouns

1. net	.....	9. forehand	.....
2. pitch	.....	10. penalty	.....
3. extra time	.....	11. court	.....
4. double fault	.....	12. tie-break	.....
5. set	.....	13. kick-off	.....
6. goal	.....	14. backhand	.....
7. score	.....	15. fault	.....
8. foul	.....		

Complete these sentences with one of the nouns in the column on the left.

a. A: What time is the ....?
   B: Eight o'clock, I think.

b. A: What's the ....?
   B: Hewitt is winning 5–3 in the first ....

c. A: Is there a tennis .... near here?
   B: Yes, there are some in the local park. They cost about £5 an hour.

d. It's been a terrible winter and the football .... is very muddy.

e. The score is still 0–0 and they're into ....

Look at the verbs below. Write F if the word is usually used to talk about football, T if it used to talk about for tennis, or B if it is used for both.

Verbs

16. score	.....	21. foul	.....
17. volley	.....	22. win	.....
18. pass	.....	23. shoot	.....
19. serve	.....	24. send off	.....
20. kick	.....		

Complete these sentences with one of the verbs above in the correct form.

f. Williams is .... for the match at 5–4, 40–15.

g. Ronaldo turns, he .... What a goal!

h. Beckham was .... after a foul on the Brazilian number five.

7 | Books and newspapers

Most people read something every day. Put the words in the box below into the two groups.

article	feature column	non-fiction
bestseller	fiction	paperback
blockbuster	front page	plot
chapter	hardback	sports section
contents page	headlines	tabloid
cover	horoscope	yesterday's
daily	index	
editorial	jobs page	

a. **Words/expressions associated with books:**

   ....
   ....

b. **Words/expressions associated with newspapers:**

   ....
   ....

Complete these sentences with words from the box on page 18.

1. I'm a Scorpio, but I never read my .... I think that's a load of rubbish.

2. The first thing I do when I get a paper is turn to the .... and check the football results.

3. I never buy novels in .... I always wait for the paperback version to come out.

4. I don't really read fiction. I prefer ....

5. There's an excellent .... at the back which helps you find just about anything in the book – it even gives paragraph numbers.

6. This must be the longest book I've ever read. I've just started .... forty-two!

8 | *Go, play* or *do*?

Complete these sentences with the correct form of *go, play* or *do*.

1. Do you .... swimming much?

2. Do you .... chess?

3. Do you .... out much?

4. A friend of mine .... karate.

5. A friend of mine .... a lot of windsurfing.

6. A friend of mine .... dancing every Friday night   it's salsa, I think.

7. I'm .... an evening class on life drawing.

8. I .... squash once a week.

9. I .... skiing as often as I can.

10. I .... a bit of weight-training.

11. Do you want to .... cards?

12. Do you want to .... skateboarding?

9 | Prepositions

Complete the sentences below with the prepositions in the box.

about	at (x2)	in	on	with

1. I quite like cycling, but I'm not very keen .... doing it for more than an hour without a stop.

2. I used to be interested .... castles and things like that when I was young, but as I got older I lost interest.

3. I'm really bad .... maths. I'm hopeless at it.

4. My sister is mad .... a certain football player! She supports Manchester United.

5. I used my new skis last weekend. They're great. I'm really pleased .... them.

6. I like watching sport, especially rugby, but I'm not very good .... playing anything.

Complete these expressions.

7. good ....

8. keen ....

9. mad ....

10. pleased ....

11. interested ....

12. bad ....

Now complete the sentences below with the expressions in the box.

annoyed with	famous for	good with	impressed by

13. Kay is really .... children. She's the ideal primary school teacher.

14. I'm .... Keith. He was late and he didn't bring the papers he said he would. He ruined the whole meeting.

15. When I actually met the Prince, I was very .... him and how relaxed he was.

16. Is it the Welsh who are .... their singing?

10 | Writing: your interests

Write about one of your interests. Answer the questions and use some of the expressions given to write your answer.

1. When did you start doing it?
   It all started when (I saw an advert for it).
   A friend of mine (persuaded me to try it).

2. Why do you like it so much?
   The reason I like it is (it's great fun).
   The best thing about it is (the people you meet).
   One day I hope to (go in for competitions).
   It helps me (keep fit).

3. How much time do you spend on it?
   Whenever I can/once a week/most weekends

4. Other comments
   The only problem with it is …
   I'd really recommend it to anyone who …

4 Unusual interests

1 -ing forms

In the conversation in the Coursebook, Dan says: 'It just got to me after a while, staying out dancing all night and then having to go to work first thing in the morning.' Make sentences by matching the beginnings 1–7 to the endings a–g.

1. It's not easy being a model, you know,
2. It's not easy being a housewife, you know,
3. It's no joke working nights, I can tell you,
4. It's quite stressful being a lorry driver, you know,
5. It's great going camping,
6. We had a brilliant time in Barbados,
7. I hate commuting,

a. getting up early, sitting in the traffic, never getting home before seven.
b. travelling all over the place, living out of a suitcase, working fourteen hours a day.
c. driving long distances, sleeping in the cab, not eating properly for days.
d. lying on the beach, swimming, trying different food. It was fantastic.
e. looking after the children, keeping the house tidy and having to cook for everyone.
f. breathing in the fresh air, cooking out in the open and sleeping under the stars.
g. going to work at ten, trying to stay awake and going to bed when everyone else is getting up.

Now underline all the *-ing* forms.

2 Paragraph ordering

Put the paragraphs A–G in the correct order to make an article about someone's very strange hobby.

Snake Charmer!

A. But I bet you don't know anyone quite like Lisa, a hotel receptionist, who spends all her free time looking after Tim, Tom and Sam – three boa constrictor snakes, which live in her bedroom.

B. Lisa Redpath doesn't have a boyfriend. She doesn't have time for one, she says, because for twenty-one-year-old Lisa, her hobby is more important than trying to find Mr Right. This is not unusual, of course. We all know people who devote evenings and weekends to their favourite pastime or sport, even when it means less time for relaxing with friends.

C. 'But what is it that takes up so much time?' I asked. 'Surely snakes just look after themselves.'

D. Most people who have snakes keep the creatures in a glass tank, but Lisa prefers to let them move around freely in her room. 'I used to keep them in a tank,' she says, 'but it seemed so unnatural, so I decided to turn my whole bedroom into a more natural habitat for them.' It was around that time that Lisa's last flatmate moved out. 'I was quite glad when she left. She was a bit strange,' said Lisa, 'and it meant I had more time to concentrate on my snakes.'

E. 'No boyfriend at the moment?' I asked, changing the subject. Lisa continued stroking Sam while she thought about the question. 'Not really. I just haven't got the time,' she sighs. 'Anyway, they don't hang around long once they meet my three boys here. Love me, love my snakes, that's what I say.'

F. I left Lisa to give Tim, Tom and Sam their dinner, closing the door very firmly behind me.

G. 'They need a lot of talking to and affection,' she replied. 'It keeps them calm, otherwise they get agitated. They also need a regular supply of mice, otherwise they get hungry and very moody. I'm often down at the pet shop for mice or rats.' She sat there looking at me as if she had said something perfectly normal, while I tried not to be sick.

The correct order is: ....

3 | Otherwise

In Exercise 2, paragraph G, you read: 'They also need a regular supply of mice, otherwise they get hungry and very moody.' Make sentences by matching the beginnings 1–6 to the endings a–f.

1. I'd better go to bed soon, otherwise ☐

2. Give me a ring if you know you're going to be late, otherwise ☐

3. We'd better let the neighbours know we're having a party, otherwise ☐

4. I'm going to have to start eating less rubbish, otherwise ☐

5. I'm going to have to start cutting down on my spending, otherwise ☐

6. I need a few cups of strong coffee in the morning, otherwise ☐

a. I'll be standing there waiting for you.

b. I just don't wake up properly and I can't think straight.

c. I'll be tired in the morning.

d. I'm going to get into serious debt.

e. they'll get annoyed with all the noise.

f. I'm going to get fat.

4 | More -ing forms (CB page 26)

Can you remember which -ing form verb completes these sentences from the text in Exercise 2?

1. Her hobby is more important than . . . . to find Mr Right.

2. Even when it means less time for . . . . with friends.

3. (Lisa) spends all her free time . . . . Tim, Tom and Sam.

4. They need a lot of . . . . to and affection.

5. She sat there . . . . at me as if she had said something perfectly normal, while I tried not to be sick.

6. 'No boyfriend at the moment?' I asked, ... the subject.

7. I left Lisa to give Tim, Tom and Sam their dinner, ... the door very firmly behind me.

5 | Need + -ing

Look at the pattern in this sentence:

This room needs tidying.

Look at the pictures below and say what needs doing using the verbs in the box.

clean	iron	paint	sign
do	mend	plug in	wash

1. The tap needs

. . . .

2. The wall needs

. . . .

3. My glasses need

. . . .

4. The dishes need

. . . .

5. The lead needs

. . . .

6. My shirt needs

. . . .

7. This letter needs

. . . .

8. Our car needs

. . . .

6 Prepositions (CB page 28)

The extract below is from the text 'It's a man's world' on page 28 of the Coursebook. Complete it with the prepositions in the box.

against	from	of (x2)
for	in (x3)	on

However, several recent news stories have highlighted the fact that women are still being discriminated (1) .... in all areas (2) .... life. A survey last year showed that (3) .... average women earn 30% less than men and that (4) .... many companies, there is still a glass ceiling, preventing women (5) .... getting the top jobs. As if this wasn't bad enough, evidence also suggests that women do more than their fair share of the work (6) .... the home. Women today have the burden (7) .... having to go out and fight (8) .... their rights (9) .... the workplace – and are then still expected to come home and cook and clean.

7 Abbreviations (CB page 28)

In the text about Jane Crouch on page 28 of the Coursebook, you read the letters BBBC, which stand for the British Boxing Board of Control. Do you know what these more common abbreviations stand for?

1. ASAP ....
2. fao ....
3. PTO ....
4. RSVP ....
5. info ....
6. min ....
7. max ....
8. dept ....
9. approx ....
10. c/o ....
11. arr ....
12. dep ....
13. eta ....
14. e.g. ....
15. tba ....
16. tbc ....

These abbreviations are common in e-mails. What do they stand for?

17. fyi ....
18. btw ....
19. cc ....
20. bcc ....
21. lol ....

8 Collocations: *decision* (CB page 31)

Complete the sentences below with the correct form of the verbs in the box.

announce	make
approve of	overturn
face with	put it off
live with	vindicate

1. On my birthday my brother and his girlfriend .... their decision to get engaged to the whole family. We were all delighted!

2. We all have to take a pay cut. Obviously, no one's happy about the decision, but we're just going to have to .... it, if we want to stay working here.

3. We think our neighbour's involved with drugs and we're .... a very difficult decision – do we tell the police or not?

4. I know you don't .... my decision to emigrate to New Zealand, but it's my life and it's up to me to decide what I do with it.

5. Stop um-ing and ah-ing and .... a decision. It's not difficult!

6. Some of the best-paid jobs around at the moment are for people who know two or more languages, which .... my decision to study Chinese – everybody thought I was mad.

7. I'm sorry to tell you that the decision we reached at our last meeting was .... by the executive.

8. Sooner or later, you've got to decide whether you want to marry me or not. You can't keep .... for ever!

9 Words ending in *-ism*

The text 'It's a man's world' on page 28 of the Coursebook described the sexism still facing women in the workplace today. Match the words ending in *-ism* 1–8 to the descriptions a–h.

1. ageism ☐
2. atheism ☐
3. capitalism ☐
4. consumerism ☐
5. plagiarism ☐
6. racism ☐
7. socialism ☐
8. terrorism ☐

a. The belief that there is no God.
b. Taking work written by another person and using it as your own.
c. The belief that some races are superior to others.
d. An economic system in which private businesses compete against each other and aim to make a profit for themselves, not for the state.
e. The use of violence for political aims.
f. Treating older people unfairly, considering them to be too old to be of use.
g. The belief that people benefit from buying and using a large quantity of goods.
h. A political ideology based on the belief that a country's natural resources and industries should be owned and controlled by the state, and that wealth should be distributed equally to all citizens of the state.

Notice the words we use for the people who believe in or carry out the above: *racist, terrorist, capitalist, socialist, atheist, plagiarist.* (You will probably not meet *ageist* as a noun, although you may meet it as an adjective: 'That's such an ageist point of view.' The people who make *consumerism* work are *consumers* – people who buy things.)

10 Writing: an article

While browsing an English language learning website, you see this invitation to write an article.

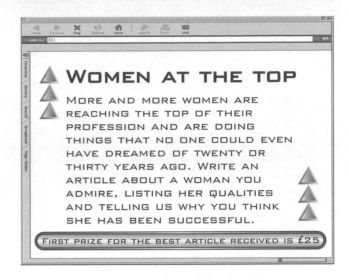

> ## WOMEN AT THE TOP
>
> MORE AND MORE WOMEN ARE REACHING THE TOP OF THEIR PROFESSION AND ARE DOING THINGS THAT NO ONE COULD EVEN HAVE DREAMED OF TWENTY OR THIRTY YEARS AGO. WRITE AN ARTICLE ABOUT A WOMAN YOU ADMIRE, LISTING HER QUALITIES AND TELLING US WHY YOU THINK SHE HAS BEEN SUCCESSFUL.
>
> FIRST PRIZE FOR THE BEST ARTICLE RECEIVED IS £25

Sample article
Complete the article below with the correct form of the verbs in the box.

beat	expect	have	meet
challenge	give	lead	respect

Senior manager and great squash player

It's amazing to think that today there are still men who believe that top management should be an all-male domain. I (1) . . . . anyone who thinks women are not capable of being a top manager to meet my boss. I have never met anyone with so much energy and enthusiasm for everything she does. Here are just some of her qualities: focused, decisive, knowledgeable, open to new ideas, approachable, honest. Perhaps her strongest quality as a boss is the fact that she (2) . . . . by example; she doesn't just (3) . . . . orders and then (4) . . . . everyone to jump!

Although she is approachable and very friendly, she definitely (5) . . . . a tough side to her – you know who's in charge – but she has everyone's respect and loyalty. One thing she's very proud of is that she is the best squash player in the company – she (6) . . . . all the men and she loves it. It's great to watch.

I think she's so successful because she just has a great way with people. The moment you (7) . . . . her, you like and (8) . . . . her, and you want to be a part of her team. And the more you get to know and work with her, the more impressive she gets. Quite an amazing woman!

Now write an article about a woman you admire and respect.

5 Big decisions

1 Giving explanations: past perfect continuous

Match the questions 1–6 to the responses a–f.

1. So how come you stopped playing football? ☐
2. Why did you decide to move out of London? ☐
3. So why did you decide to quit your job? ☐
4. You lived in Russia for a few years, didn't you? How come? ☐
5. So why did you split up with Brian? ☐
6. What made you think of doing a marathon – at your age? You must be crazy! ☐

a. We hadn't been getting on for a while. I felt we'd just reached the end of the road.

b. Well, I'd been working for the BBC in different parts of eastern Europe and I got moved to Moscow in 1989.

c. Well, I'd been having a lot of trouble with my back, and we seemed to be losing every week so I just decided to stop.

d. Well, I'd been wanting to do something a bit mad for years. I'm glad I did it. It gave me a great sense of achievement.

e. I'd just had enough. I'd been waiting for a promotion for a couple of years and when it didn't come I just decided it was time to move on.

f. Oh. Well, I didn't want to, but my girlfriend had been nagging me about living so far away, so I just moved a bit closer to her, that's all.

Go back and underline the past perfect continuous in the responses above.

2 What's the job? (CB page 38)

Which job is being described in the sentences 1–10?

bouncer	soldier
comedian	surgeon
lawyer	ticket inspector
mechanic	traffic warden
plumber	vet

1. I perform operations like taking out someone's appendix and things like that.

   ....

2. People come to me when they've got an oil leak or they need their brakes fixed.

   ....

3. I'm employed by a local club to make sure people don't cause trouble.

   ....

4. I install central heating and fix people's dripping taps.

   ....

5. I treat animals and sometimes have to put them to sleep.

   ....

6. I go through years of training so that I can defend my country.

   ....

7. I defend people who have been accused of committing a crime.

   ....

8. I make sure people have paid their fare on the train.

   ....

9. I make sure people park their cars properly. Nobody likes me.

   ....

10. I make people laugh! I work in comedy clubs doing stand-up.

    ....

3 Second conditionals (CB page 39)

Complete the sentences below with the pairs of verbs in the box.

be / could	could / can't	do / were
bother / were	die / happened	do / paid

1. A: Do you want me to pick up your photos while I'm in town?

   B: Oh, that'd .... great if you ....

2. A: Is there really no way you can come tonight? We'd really love you to.

   B: Look, I would if I ...., but I .... I've got to get this essay finished.

3. A: I was thinking of going to that new café for lunch.

   B: Oh, I wouldn't .... that if I .... you! The food there's disgusting!

4. A: I was thinking of going to see that new exhibition later.

   B: Really? I wouldn't .... if I .... you.

5. A: I decided to take up golf, you know, just to try to impress my boss.

   B: You must be mad! I wouldn't .... that if you .... me!

6. You must've been really embarrassed when you were stopped at Customs. I'd .... if that ever .... to me.

4 Wish and conditionals

Look at these sentences with wish:

I wish I had a more interesting job.
I wish John wasn't late all the time.

Notice these common patterns:

I wish I had …	I wish I lived …
I wish I knew …	I wish I were(n't) …
I wish I could …	I wish I didn't have to …

Now make sentences with wish. For example:

It's so cold.
I wish it wasn't so cold.

1. I have to work this weekend.

   I .... this weekend.

2. A holiday in the Bahamas would be nice but I can't afford it at the moment.

   I .... to go on holiday.

3. There are so many tourists here.

   I .... so many tourists here.

4. Our car's too small.

   I .... a bigger car.

5. I don't like living out in the country.

   I .... a bit nearer the city.

Look at these second conditional sentences:

If I had the money, I'd lend it to you.
If we were free, we'd call in.

Now make second conditional sentences.

6. I can't give you a lift. I haven't got my car.
   If ....

7. I can't phone him. I haven't got his number.
   I'd ....

8. I haven't got enough time to learn a foreign language.
   I'd ....

9. He doesn't speak very clearly. People don't understand what he says.
   If ....

Complete these sentences with a verb in the correct form.

10. I'm basically happy with my job, but I just wish I .... a bit more money. If I ...., it would mean we could have a holiday.

11. I wish the weather here .... better. I mean, if we .... better summers, I wouldn't need to go abroad twice a year.

12. I've got a friend of my brother's from Italy staying at the moment, but he speaks hardly any English. I just wish I .... a bit of Italian.

5 Famous conditionals

Here are five quotations. Complete them with the words in the box.

borrow	lonely	misinformed	pleasure	wolves

1. If you live among . . . . , you have to act like a wolf.

2. If you wish to be thoroughly . . . . about a country, consult a man who has lived there for thirty years and speaks the language like a native.

3. If you would like to know the value of money, go and try to . . . . some.

4. If we had no faults, we would not take so much . . . . in noticing them in others.

5. If I'm such a legend, then why am I so . . . . ? (Said by the singer Judy Garland, who, sadly, later died in tragic circumstances.)

6 Question tags (CB page 40)

In the conversation in the Coursebook, Phil says: 'It's pretty quiet down there, isn't it?' Complete these sentences with the correct question tag.

1. You are coming tomorrow, ... ?
2. You live quite near here, ... ?
3. You can speak a bit of Russian, ... ?
4. He's about forty, ... ?
5. Your parents don't like the beach, ... ?
6. It's not very warm in here, ... ?
7. Barcelona's beautiful, ... ?
8. It gets dark around seven, ... ?
9. It's not very important, ... ?
10. Macs are much better than PCs, ... ?
11. She never arrives on time, ... ?
12. She comes by bus, ... ?
13. We're meeting at eight, ... ?
14. We'll be finished by four, ... ?
15. I'm a bit early, ... ?
16. I'm meeting you at your place, ... ?

7 You don't ... , do you?

Here is a common way of asking for information or help:

You don't know anything about this party tomorrow night, do you?

Now look at these three patterns:

a. You don't ... , do you?
b. You couldn't ... , could you?
c. You haven't ... , have you?

Write a, b or c next to these phrases, depending on which pattern you would use with them.

1. know what time the chemist opens . . . . .
2. help me carry this box . . . . .
3. seen my mobile phone anywhere . . . . .
4. got a calculator . . . . .
5. lend me £10 . . . . .
6. sell batteries . . . . .
7. photocopy these for me . . . . .
8. heard anything about the train strike . . . . .
9. give me a lift . . . . .
10. know where I can cash a cheque . . . . .
11. post this for me . . . . .
12. seen my passport . . . . .

8 I knew I'd have to ...

Look at this common pattern in spoken English:

I knew I'd have to give up smoking if I wanted to be a fireman.

Make sentences by matching the beginnings 1–10 to the endings a–j.

1. I realised I'd have to apologise ☐
2. I knew I'd have to dress smartly ☐
3. I knew I'd have to get the tickets well in advance ☐
4. I realised I'd have to work a lot harder ☐
5. I knew I'd have to run ☐
6. I realised I'd have to catch the early train ☐
7. I knew I'd have to save for a while ☐
8. I realised I'd have to get a lot fitter ☐
9. I knew I'd have to get a taxi home ☐
10. I realised I'd have to buy a very expensive ring ☐

a. if I wanted the best seats.
b. if I wanted to impress them.
c. if I wanted us to remain friends.
d. if I wanted her to say yes.
e. if I wanted to pass the course.
f. if I wanted to catch the bus.
g. if I wanted to run a marathon.
h. if I wanted to be there before nine.
i. if I wanted to have a drink.
j. if I wanted to buy my own flat.

9 Stuck (CB page 40)

In the conversation, Jason says: 'I don't want to spend my life stuck in front of a computer screen.' The basic meaning of *stuck* is *can't or won't move*. Complete the sentences below with the expressions in the box.

get stuck	stuck in an office
it's stuck	stuck in traffic
stuck in a rut	stuck with it

1. I couldn't do Jane's job – . . . . all day, sitting in front of a computer.

2. Hello, Harry, it's only me. I'm . . . . , so I'll be about half an hour late.

3. I can't open the door – . . . .

4. I think I know what to do, but if I . . . . , can I give you a ring?

5. I'm so bored. I'm just . . . . , doing the same thing day after day.

6. I don't really like the colour of our new car, but I'm . . . . My husband chose it.

Most of the expressions above are idiomatic uses of *stuck*. The idiomatic use of some words is sometimes more common than the literal use. For example:

Did you see the moon last night? (literal use)
Do you see what I mean? (metaphorical use)

In the second example, *see* means *understand*.

10 It's just as well (CB page 40)

In the conversation in the Coursebook, Phil said: 'Just as well you gave up', which means 'It's a good thing you gave up'. Match the statements 1–5 to the follow-up comments a–e.

1. It's just as well you brought your umbrella. ☐
2. It's just as well you went to the cash machine. ☐
3. It's just as well you speak German. ☐
4. It's just as well we arrived early. ☐
5. It's just as well we didn't bring the children. ☐

a. I got the time of the train wrong.

b. Nobody here seems to speak English at all.

c. This place is expensive.

d. It was a much scarier film than I thought.

e. I think it's going to start raining.

Now make short dialogues by matching the comments 6–10 to the responses f–j.

6. My mobile needs re-charging. It's dead. ☐
7. Tim, it's me. The meeting's been cancelled. ☐
8. I'm too tired to go out tonight. Do you mind? ☐
9. I forgot to tell Gina about the party. ☐
10. I've bought a tie for Paul's birthday. ☐

f. It's just as well you didn't. She isn't invited.

g. It's just as well I've got mine, then.

h. It's just as well you rang me. I was about to leave.

i. It's just as well you told me. I was going to buy him one myself.

j. No, it's probably just as well. I've got a cold coming on.

> **Real English:** *it's a good job …*
>
> Another way to say *it's just as well* is *it's a good job*.
> *It's a good job you speak German.*
> *It's a good job you rang me.*
> *It's a good job we booked early.*
> *It's a good job you rang first.*

11 Encouraging expressions

Make expressions which encourage people to make decisions and take action. Put the words in the right order. Begin as shown.

1. it's / a / worth / try
   It's . . . .

2. you've / to / lose / nothing / got
   You've . . . .

3. unless / know / try / you / you'll / never
   You'll . . . .

4. it's / never / now / or
   It's . . . .

5. a / cake / of / piece / it's
   It's . . . .

6. there's / out / way / to / only / find / one
   There's . . . .

7. happen / could / the / worst / what's / that / ?
   What's . . . . ?

12 Collocations

**Make sentences by matching the beginnings 1–8 to the endings a–h
that collocate best.**

1. I decided to leave
2. I decided to take
3. I decided to hand in
4. I decided to take up
5. I decided to stop
6. I decided to move
7. I decided to do
8. I decided to change

a. a year off and travel.
b. being so negative about everything.
c. golf.
d. nothing about it.
e. house.
f. careers completely.
g. home and find a flat.
h. my notice at work.

13 Why? How come?

Complete these sentences with *why* or *how come*.

1. So . . . . you didn't finish your university course?
2. So . . . . you can afford a new car? Have you had a pay rise or something?
3. So . . . . did you decide to leave home so young? I mean, sixteen is very young, isn't it?
4. So . . . . you and Andy aren't going to Spain now? I thought you'd definitely decided to go?
5. So . . . . did you decide to study in England? I mean, why not the US or Australia?
6. So . . . . aren't you coming round next weekend? Have you changed your plans?
7. So . . . . you've never been on a plane? Are you scared of flying or something?
8. So . . . . did your parents decide to move to Scotland? Was it because of a job or something?

Notice also these common questions:
What made you decide to become a doctor?
What made you decide to go to the University of Wales?

14 Writing: a letter

**Write a letter to a friend telling him or her about a big decision you have made.
Before you write, read the example letter. Try to use the language in bold.**

> **Dear** Pete,
>
> **Thanks for your last letter. It was good to hear all your news. The big news
> from me is** that Rebecca and I have **decided** to get married. We've only known
> each other for six months, but we've **thought it about carefully** and **talked it
> through**, so we're going into it with our **eyes wide open**. We're both thirty-five, so
> at least nobody can tell us we're being young and silly, although, I must admit, I still
> occasionally stop and ask myself if we really are **doing the right thing** – but that's
> only natural, isn't it?
>
> Both sets of parents are very excited. We're **planning to** get married in the summer
> – probably some time in July. I hope you'll be free to come. We're **hoping to** sell
> both our flats and buy a bigger place somewhere outside town. **I'll ring you when**
> we've fixed the date.
>
> **All the best,**
> Roger

6 Flying

1 Airports and planes

Complete the first part of the text below with the words in the box.

board	departure lounge
boarding	passport control
check-in desk	screens
delay	trolley
departure gate	

The first thing I do when I get to the airport is get a (1) . . . . for my luggage. Then I find out which (2) . . . . to go to and check in. The first thing I ask is: 'Is there a (3) . . . . ?' The longest I've ever been stuck at an airport was twenty-six hours – coming home from Delhi! After that, I go straight through (4) . . . . into the (5) . . . . and get something to eat and look round the shops. I try to sit somewhere where I can see the TV (6) . . . . to see when my flight is (7) . . . . I usually wait till the last minute before going to the (8) . . . . I'm usually the last one to (9) . . . .

Now complete the second part of the text with the words in the box.

airline	flier	landing	reclaim
Customs	hand	locker	window

I always ask for a(n) (10) . . . . seat on the plane. I like to see where I'm going! I'm not really a nervous (11) . . . . , so take-off and (12) . . . . don't worry me. If it's a long flight, I try to have a sleep on the plane if I can, usually after the meal. Unlike most people, I like (13) . . . . meals.

As soon as the plane lands, I get my (14) . . . . luggage out of the overhead (15) . . . . and try to get off the plane quickly so I can get to the baggage (16) . . . . area and get a trolley – there are never enough. After that, it's just (17) . . . . and, thankfully, I've never been stopped there.

On a plane there are *window seats*, *aisle seats*, and *middle seats*. The *aisle* is the corridor between the rows of seats. *Aisle* is pronounced like *I'll*.

Language note

On a plane there are *window seats*, *aisle seats*, and *middle seats*. The *aisle* is the corridor between the rows of seats. *Aisle* is pronounced like *I'll*.

2 Idioms focus

In the text on page 43 of the Coursebook, the anti-smoking lobby were pleased that Ms Norrish was punished for smoking on a plane and said the judgement was 'a step in the right direction'. There are many idioms connected with movement and direction.

Complete the idioms in the sentences below with the words in the box.

bridge	light	step
corner	nowhere	turning
end	road	way

1. Life is full of surprises. You never know what might be just round the . . . .

2. We bought a house last year. We've spent a lot of money modernising it and it looks great, but there's still a long . . . . to go before it's finished.

3. I don't think I can stay in this job much longer. I've just reached the end of the . . . . I need a fresh start somewhere.

4. I can't say I've enjoyed my course at college, but there's only about six months left now, so the . . . . is in sight.

5. I've applied for at least forty jobs since I graduated and I haven't had one interview. I'm going . . . . fast. Why did I bother going to university?

6. So, you're getting married? Well, that's it then. There's no . . . . back now. Good luck! You'll need it!

7. You don't need to understand the whole process straightaway. Just take it one . . . . at a time and you'll be fine.

8. We may need to give you a bit of training to help you in a few aspects of your job, but let's wait and see – we'll cross that . . . . when we come to it.

9. I've been working on this essay now for two weeks and finally I think I know what I'm doing, so at last there's . . . . at the end of the tunnel.

Now look at the answer key and check your answers.

Make the idioms by putting the words in the correct order. This will help you remember them.

a. corner / around / the / just

....

b. long / still / a / way / to / go / there's

....

c. end / of / the / reached / the road / I've

....

d. sight / the / is / end / in

....

e. nowhere / I'm / fast / going

....

f. turning / no / back / there's

....

g. one / at / a / step / time

....

h. we'll / bridge / that / cross / when / we / come / to / it

....

i. light / at / the / tunnel / there's / end / of / the

....

Joke

A: It's been difficult, but there's light at the end of the tunnel!

B: Sure, but have you thought it may be a train coming in the opposite direction?

---

3 Phrasal verbs with *up* (CB page 43)

Joan Norrish got into trouble for trying to *light up* on a plane. Complete the sentences below with the correct form of the verbs in the box.

bottle	freshen	pick	split
come	make	set	turn

1. I've decided to give up smoking. That's it. I've .... up my mind.

2. No, I'm joking. I don't really speak Swedish. I just .... up a few expressions while I was on holiday there.

3. Did you hear Jackie's .... up with her boyfriend again? That's the third time this month! She says she's had enough!

4. A: Did you play volleyball on Sunday?

   B: Yes, but it wasn't very good. Only five people .... up.

5. I'm afraid I'm going to have to cancel going out tonight. A problem's .... up.

6. I'll meet you back here at seven. That gives me an hour to go home and .... up.

7. It's not healthy to .... up your feelings. You've got to learn to express your emotions – otherwise you'll get ill or something.

8. I need to .... up an e-mail account for my sister. I'm fed up with her using mine.

---

4 Comparatives (CB page 45)

Complete the sentences below with the comparative form of the adjectives in the box.

easy	good	mild	tough
expensive	interesting	old	young

1. The opera tickets were much .... than I thought they would be, but I still decided to get them.

2. England was much .... than I'd expected. I didn't need my jumpers at all.

3. Skiing is much .... than I'd expected. After only one lesson I was actually doing it without falling!

4. The journey was much .... than I'd expected. The roads were really clear.

5. Getting a job here is much .... than I thought it would be. Everybody seems to be looking for one.

6. His wife is much .... than I'd expected. In fact, he's almost old enough to be her father.

7. English lessons are much .... than I thought they would be. It's because the teacher is so lively.

8. Your children are much .... than I'd expected. I thought they were still at school.

5 Absolutely (CB page 45)

We often use *very* with normal adjectives and *absolutely* with stronger adjectives. For example:

It's very hot in here.
It's absolutely boiling in here.

Match the adjectives 1–10 to stronger ones a–j.

1.	cold	a.	tiny
2.	tired	b.	enormous
3.	big	c.	devastated
4.	small	d.	exhausted
5.	tasty	e.	brilliant
6.	pleased	f.	delicious
7.	disappointed	g.	delighted
8.	frightened	h.	fascinating
9.	interesting	i.	freezing
10.	good	j.	terrified

Now complete these short dialogues with *absolutely* and a strong adjective from above. The first one has been done for you.

11. A: It's cold today, isn't it?
    B: Yes, it's *absolutely freezing*.

12. A: Did you stay in one of those big hotels?
    B: Yes, it was . . . .

13. A: Are you pleased with your exam results?
    B: Yes, I'm . . . .

14. A: You failed again! You must be disappointed.
    B: Yes, I was . . . . when I found out.

15. A: You went to the theatre last night, didn't you? Was it any good?
    B: Yes, it was . . . .

16. A: There was a really interesting programme last night about monkeys on BBC 1.
    B: Yes, I saw that. It was . . . ., wasn't it?

17. A: I thought that car was going to hit you. I was really frightened.
    B: You were frightened! I was . . . .!

18. A: Mm. This soup's tasty, isn't it?
    B: Yes, it's . . . .

19. A: Are you tired? You certainly look it.
    B: Tired? I'm . . . .

20. A: What about your hotel? Was it OK?
    B: No, the rooms were . . . ., just enough room for a bed and nothing else!

6 Infinitive or *-ing* form 1 (CB page 46)

Complete these sentences with the infinitive or the *-ing* form of the verbs in brackets.

1. Ed's finally admitted . . . . the money from my desk. (take)

2. We can afford . . . . abroad on holiday this year. (go)

3. I never agreed . . . . with you. You obviously misunderstood. (come)

4. We aim . . . . at your place around three o'clock in the afternoon. (arrive)

5. We've all arranged . . . . at six at the station. (meet)

6. You can't avoid . . . . mistakes when you're learning a foreign language. (make)

7. Have you ever considered . . . . and . . . . abroad? (live, work)

8. I've decided not . . . . out tonight. I'm too tired. (go)

9. I managed . . . . Jim and Mary to come with us. (persuade)

10. If you work hard at your studies, you deserve . . . . (succeed)

11. I don't really fancy . . . . to the airport. Shall we get a taxi? (drive)

12. I'm afraid I failed . . . . Martin to change his mind. (persuade)

13. Once I've finished . . . . my homework, I'll call you. (do)

14. Sorry, I completely forgot . . . . your letter. (post)

15. I'm hoping . . . . mid-morning. Is that OK? (arrive)

16. I love London. I can't imagine . . . . anywhere else. (live)

7 Infinitive or -ing form 2 (CB page 46)

Complete these sentences with the infinitive or the -ing form of the verbs in brackets.

1. My job involves . . . . to the Far East a lot. (travel)

2. Where did you learn . . . . such good English? (speak)

3. Do you fancy . . . . for a pizza later? (go)

4. Mark and Ruth have offered . . . . me to 'Les Miserables'. (take)

5. I'm planning . . . . the early train in the morning. (catch)

6. My Spanish is getting better but I need to practise . . . . more. (speak)

7. I promise . . . . you as soon as I get to my hotel. (phone)

8. I'm sorry but I refuse . . . . all weekend watching you play football. (spend)

9. We risk . . . . soaked to the skin if we leave now. Just look at those clouds! (get)

10. I usually stop work around eleven o'clock . . . . a coffee. (have)

11. He stopped . . . . professional football five years ago. (play)

12. The local authority is threatening . . . . the village school again. (close)

13. Still no answer? Try . . . . him again at home. (phone)

14. Sorry I didn't phone you. I tried . . . . a phone but there wasn't one around. (find)

15. We stopped . . . . a bite to eat at a motorway service station. (have)

16. They've stopped us . . . . personal calls at work. (make)

Did you notice the different structure after stop in 10, 11, 15 and 16 above?

8 Quick verb check

Circle the verbs which are followed by infinitives and underline those which are followed by -ing forms. Then check your answers in the answer key.

admit	deny	imagine	
agree	deserve	involve	promise
aim	fail	learn	refuse
arrange	fancy	manage	risk
avoid	finish	offer	threaten
consider	hope	practise	

9 Expressions with in

Complete the short dialogues below with the expressions in the box.

in a hurry	in particular	in practice
in a minute	in public	in time
in common	in the end	in trouble
in general	in theory	

1. A: You don't seem to spend much time with your brother, do you?

   B: Well, we don't have much . . . .

2. A: Are you ready?

   B: Not quite. I'll be with you . . . .

3. A: Clare, can I just ask you something?

   B: Sorry, not now. I'm . . . .

4. A: Did you have a good time in London?

   B: Brilliant! We arrived just . . . . to see a royal procession – a wedding, I think.

5. A: I was sorry to hear Jason's lost his job.

   B: Yes, his company's . . . . They've just made fifty people redundant.

6. A: Are you doing anything over the weekend?

   B: Nothing . . . . Why?

7. A: So, you had to take it back to the shop three times? That's crazy!

   B: I know! . . . . , I just asked for my money back.

8. A: You're going to Brussels via Eurostar?

   B: Yes, ... I prefer to fly, but I thought it would make a change and it's just as quick.

9. A: Have you ever had to make a speech, Tony?

   B: No, I don't like speaking . . . .

10. A: What do you think of my idea, then?

    B: It's a good idea . . . . , but I don't think it'll work . . . .

10 Expressions with *mind*

Do you sometimes have trouble *making up your mind*? Complete the short dialogues below with the expressions in the box.

> I changed my mind
> I haven't made up my mind
> I'll bear that in mind
> it completely slipped my mind
> never mind
> nowhere springs to mind
> you must be out of your mind

1. A: What are you doing here? I thought you were going into the town centre?

   B: I was, but . . . .

2. A: You said you were going to phone last night.

   B: I know. I'm sorry. . . . .

3. A: If you're going to phone Sally, she's usually in her office between nine and eleven.

   B: Thanks. . . . .

4. A: Are you going to Ireland again this year?

   B: I don't know. I might go Scotland. . . . . yet.

5. A: I think we've just missed a train.

   B: . . . . We've got plenty of time.

6. A: Can you think of somewhere we could go for a weekend break?

   B: Not really. . . . .

7. A: We've decided to drive to India.

   B: . . . . !

Next time your teacher asks you to think of a word or an example, you could say: 'Nothing springs to mind.' Try it in the next lesson!

Can you translate the expressions in the box above into your language?

11 Writing: a formal letter

Sample formal letter
You work for a travel company and have just finalised the travel arrangements for a group of English students who are going on a school trip to Spain. Write to the group leader, informing her of flight times and airport transfers.

Task I
Choose the correct word.

Dear Mrs Stevens,

Please find (1) *included / enclosed* the travel documents for you and your party of sixteen students, travelling to Madrid on Saturday, 18 March 2003. I am pleased to be able to confirm your (2) *total / full* travel details below.

Your flight number is BA 449, departing from London Gatwick at 14.30. We recommend you arrive at the airport and check in two hours before the flight is (3) *expected / due* to depart. The flight arrives in Madrid at 17.45 (4) *local / area* time. You will be met in the Arrivals Lounge by one of our representatives, who will be holding a (5) *sign / notice* with your school name. From there, you will travel by coach to your hotel, the Castello Royale. Transfer time is (6) *nearly / approximately* 45 minutes.

Your hotel reservation is for nine rooms for seven nights. We (7) *regret / announce* that any cancellations cannot be (8) *refunded / returned* at this late stage.

Your return details on Saturday, 25 March, are as follows. Flight number BA 450 departing Madrid at 16.45, arriving at London Gatwick at 18.00. Please be ready in the hotel lobby for a (9) *prompt / quick* departure by coach at 14.00.

Thank you again for using us to arrange your travel details, and may I take this (10) *chance / opportunity* to wish you an enjoyable stay in Madrid. Please do not (11) *hesitate / wait* to contact me if we can assist you (12) *more / further* in any way.

Yours (13) *sincerely / faithfully*,

Xavier Lopez

Task 2
Now write a formal letter to Mr Peterson, confirming the details of the trip below. Use the letter above as a model.

Mr Peterson
Party: 12 students
Destination: Rome

Flight details out:
Dep. London Heathrow.
Friday, May 12, 12.35, BA 229
Arr. Rome, 15.55

Flight details home:
Dep. Rome, Tuesday, May 16, 13.30,
BA 241
Arr. London Heathrow, 14.50

Transfers: will be met at airport.
3 taxis, direct to hotel. transfer time:
approx. 1 hour
Hotel: Hotel Britannia: 7 rooms for
4 nights

1 Future arrangements (CB page 50)

In the Coursebook, Ken told Steve about his plans to go to a party on a boat. He said: 'I'm going to my friends Pete and Rachel's party.'

Complete part of their conversation with suitable verbs in the present continuous. The verbs you need are in the box below the conversation. Look at them only when you have finished.

Steve: So, who (1) .... you .... to the party with? Samantha?

Ken: No, she (2) .... away for the weekend. I hope my brother's going to come with me. He (3) .... late tomorrow evening, but hopefully he'll be able to make it.

Steve: Oh right. (4) .... they .... any food at the party or what?

Ken: Well, no. Everybody (5) .... food to share. You know, to keep the cost down.

Steve: Yes, right. What (6) .... you ...., then?

Ken: A big bowl of salad.

Steve: And why (7) .... they actually .... a party? (8) .... they .... engaged or something?

Ken: Yes, they (9) .... married next year.

get (x2)   go (x2)   have (x2)   take (x2)   work

Language note

Remember that the differences between the different futures in English can be very small and difficult to explain. Here are good typical examples of each.
That's Jane. I'll let her in.
Next week's Easter, so there won't be a class.
It's minus five. It's going to snow again tonight.
The train leaves in twenty minutes.
Are you going to the meeting tonight?

2 Will/won't

We often use question tags with *will/won't* to remind people about things. For example:

You won't forget to post my letter, will you?
You will remember to post my letter, won't you?

Complete these sentences with *will* or *won't*.

1. I'm planning a secret birthday party for Patrick. You .... tell him, ... you?
2. See you at eight o'clock, then. You .... be late, ... you?
3. Have a good journey. You .... phone me when you arrive, ... you?
4. You .... ask me if you need help, ... you?
5. You .... forget to go to the bank, ... you?
6. I haven't got my key. You .... be there when I get home, ... you?
7. You .... drive home if you have anything to drink tonight, ... you?
8. You .... come and visit me in Paris, ... you?

3 *Going to* and *'ll* (CB page 49)

Complete these short dialogues with *going to* or *'ll* and the verbs in brackets.

1. A: I'm going to eat lunch outside.
   B: Good idea. I think I .... you. (join)
2. A: What's the matter? You look terrible.
   B: I feel dreadful. I think I .... sick. (be)
3. A: Can I get you a drink?
   B: I .... a coke, please. (have)
4. A: How does this drinks machine work?
   B: It's easy. I .... you.. (show)
5. A: Can I use your phone to call a taxi?
   B: Don't be silly. I .... you a lift. (give)
6. A: I'm nearly ready. Just give me five minutes.
   B: Oh, look at the time! I didn't realise it was so late. We .... late if we don't leave now. (be)
7. A: Have you e-mailed David Kemp yet?
   B: No, I've thought about it and I .... him instead. It'd be better to have a word with him. (phone)

4 Asking about plans

Make questions about someone's plans by putting the words in the correct order.

1. anything / are / doing / you / this / weekend / ?
   Are ....

2. up / you / are / to / this / what / weekend/ ?
   What ....

3. any / got / plans / you / the / weekend / for / have / ?
   Have ....

4. are / nice / weekend / you / doing / anything / this / ?
   Are ....

5. plans / holiday / have / any / got / you / ?
   Have ....

6. this / you / year / planning / go / are / away / to / ?
   Are ....

Now make answers by putting the words in the correct order. Begin as shown.

7. No. do / you / ask / why / ?
   No. ....

8. Oh, / special / nothing – about / how / you / ?
   Oh, ...

9. really / decided / yet / I / haven't
   ....

10. No. afford / it / I / can't / really / year / this
    No. ....

5 Collocations: *meeting, appointment, date* (CB page 52)

Which word, *meeting, appointment* or *date*, do these groups of verbs collocate with? (All the verbs in each group must collocate.)

1. arrange, change, confirm, decide on, make, set, fix
   a(n) ....

2. miss, cancel, fail to turn up for, break, keep, make
   a(n) ....

3. arrange, miss, have, attend, open, close, take part in, cancel a(n) ....

Which word, *meeting, appointment* or *date*, do these groups of adjectives collocate with? (All the adjectives in each group must collocate.)

4. emergency, routine, regular, dentist's, hospital
   ....

5. successful, annual, fruitful, hostile, noisy, committee, board ....

6. (in)convenient, definite, provisional, final, blind, agreed
   ....

Now complete these sentences with *meeting, appointment* or *date*.

7. That was a very successful ....

8. Let's make a provisional .... for next Monday and if it's not convenient, you can phone me, OK?

9. Mary's up at the hospital, but don't worry, it's just a routine ....

10. I'd like to open the .... by welcoming you all here today.

11. I'm afraid I need to change the .... again for your visit to Head Office. Sorry.

12. So that's Monday 4th November. I'll confirm that .... in writing next week.

13. The .... was a disaster. It was hostile from the start and then it got quite noisy as people starting shouting.

14. I'm phoning to cancel my .... with Dr Kemp. I'm afraid my car won't start.

Language note

Collocation is not like grammar. Grammar has rules which can be helpful to learn. Giving rules for collocation is not helpful. The way you learn collocations is by meeting them as often as possible.

6 Reading: future forms (CB page 49)

This short text is about Matt Surrenden and his friends. They are planning to cycle to France to raise money for charity.

First match the verbs 1–5 to the words and phrases a–e.

1. face   a. for Dover
2. continue   b. via the Tunnel
3. lead   c. the steep climb
4. start   d. a team
5. head   e. in London

Now complete the first part of the text with the phrases you formed, putting the verbs in the correct form.

Uphill all the way for Cancer Research

Local gym instructor Matt Surrenden will have to be very fit next week as he (6) . . . . of cyclists on their own tour de France to raise money for a new radiography unit at Hurst's Hospital in Surrey. The tour (7) . . . . , (8) . . . . and (9) . . . . , all the way down to Grenoble in South East France. Matt and his four friends then (10) . . . . of Alpe d'Huez, the most famous mountain section of the Tour de France. If they make it, the five intend to have a day's skiing before catching a train home.

Now complete the second part of the text with the phrases in the box. All the phrases express a future idea.

bound to	determined to	expect to	hopes to

The whole trip should take five days. 'We're (11) . . . . have a puncture or two but we're well-prepared. Five days should be plenty,' insists Matt. Each member of the team (12) . . . . raise a thousand pounds for the hospital. 'None of us has ever done anything like this before,' said Matt, 'It's not going to be easy but we're (13) . . . . enjoy ourselves as well as raise a lot of money. We also (14) . . . . be a lot fitter,' he laughed.

Real English: *an uphill struggle*

The title of the text was 'Uphill all the way'. *It's an uphill struggle* is a common expression in English. It means that the job or task you are doing is very difficult because you are experiencing a lot of problems.

A: *I can't get the management team to accept my ideas.*
B: *I know what you mean. It's always an uphill struggle to get people to change the way they do things.*

7 Myself (CB page 50)

In the conversation in the Coursebook, Steve said: 'I went to a party there myself.' Match the questions and comments 1–6 to the responses a–f.

1. Have you seen the new VW? I love it. ☐
2. We went to that new café-bar in town last night. It's actually quite nice. ☐
3. Sorry, but I don't think I'm going to have time to help you with your homework. ☐
4. Golf's great. It's really fun, really relaxing. ☐
5. Have you ever tried windsurfing? ☐
6. Do you want to come down to the beach after class? We're all going. ☐

a. No. A lot of my friends have, but I've never actually done it myself.
b. Don't worry. I'm sure I can do it myself.
c. No thanks. I'm not a beach person myself.
d. Right. I don't play myself, so I wouldn't know.
e. Really? I must go there myself some time, then.
f. Do you? I don't really like it myself.

Real English: *I'm not a beach person myself*

Here are some more examples:
I'm not a very sporty person myself.
I'm not an opera person myself.

8 Going to have to

Make sentences by matching the beginnings 1–10 to the endings a–j.

1. I'm not going to finish this essay today, so I'm going to have to ☐
2. If you want a ticket for the concert, you're going to have to ☐
3. If I want to do a marathon this year, I'm going to have to ☐
4. I haven't got any cash, so I'm going to have to ☐
5. If you want to lose weight, you're going to have to ☐
6. If I want to get a better job, I'm going to have to ☐
7. If you really want to improve your English, you're going to have to ☐
8. There's no plane on Saturday night, so we're going to have to ☐

a. phone up straightaway.
b. start training for it.
c. work over the weekend.
d. stay till Sunday.
e. pay by credit card.
f. cut down on fatty foods.
g. do an extra training course.
h. read a lot more.

8 Party animals

1 Try and …

Remember the example: 'I'll try and bring some crisps.' Make short dialogues by matching the statements and questions 1–6 to the responses a–f.

1. I don't think Paul really wants to come camping with us. ☐
2. My computer keeps crashing. ☐
3. We've run out of milk. ☐
4. When will Mrs Jones be back in the office? ☐
5. If we're going to go camping, we're going to need a tent. ☐
6. The T-shirt's fine, but the jeans are too small. ☐

a. I'll try and have a look at it later.
b. I'll try and get some when I'm out.
c. I'll try and persuade him.
d. I'll try and find a bigger pair.
e. I'll try and find out. Hold the line please.
f. I'll try and borrow one from someone at work.

2 Time prepositions: *at, on, in*

Complete the sentences below with the words and expressions in the box.

2009	March
a few minutes	4th March
about an hour	Monday morning
Christmas	Saturday
four o'clock	the summer
lunchtime	the weekend

1. It'll be ready at . . . .
   It'll be ready at . . . .
   It'll be ready at . . . .
   It'll be ready at . . . .

2. It'll be ready on . . . .
   It'll be ready on . . . .
   It'll be ready on . . . .

3. It'll be ready in . . . .
   It'll be ready in . . . .
   It'll be ready in . . . .
   It'll be ready in . . . .
   It'll be ready in . . . .

Look at the calendar below.
If today is Monday 14th May, what is the date …

4. the day after tomorrow? . . . .
5. in three days' time? . . . .
6. in a fortnight? . . . .
7. a week today? . . . .
8. a week tomorrow? . . . .
9. a fortnight tomorrow? . . . .
10. the day before yesterday? . . . .
11. not this Thursday but the Thursday after? . . . .
12. this Wednesday? . . . .
13. next Wednesday? . . . .

MAY

Monday	Tuesday	Wednesday	Thursday	Friday	Saturday	Sunday
	1	2	3	4	5	6
7	8	9	10	11	12	13
14	15	16	17	18	19	20
21	22	23	24	25	26	27
28	29	30	31			

3 It's a great place

Look at these three patterns:

a. It's a great place for a(n) …
b. It's a great place to …
c. It's a great place for …

Which words go with each pattern? Write a, b or c next to each word.

1. winter holiday . . . . .
2. teenagers . . . . .
3. quiet picnic . . . . .
4. party . . . . .
5. night out . . . . .
6. study . . . . .
7. windsurfing . . . . .
8. meet people . . . . .
9. work . . . . .
10. children . . . . .
11. meal . . . . .
12. eat . . . . .
13. food . . . . .
14. live . . . . .
15. visit . . . . .
16. explore . . . . .
17. opera lovers . . . . .
18. day-trip . . . . .

Notice that the words *holiday* and *picnic* can also be used as verbs in English.
We usually holiday in Majorca in May.
We used to picnic in that field before they built houses there.

4 Verb collocations

Go to page 56 in the Coursebook and read paragraph 3 of the text 'Rave to the grave' again. Then try to complete the extract below from memory.

The Government is already considering
(1) .... a new law which will help police
(2) .... unofficial gatherings of this kind.
They are (3) .... a bill which will
(4) .... police to (5) .... any
groups of more than twenty people listening to
'music with repetitive beats' and also intend to
(6) .... club owners responsible for any
drugs being sold on the premises. A spokesman
for the Metropolitan Police said, 'Things are
(7) .... out of hand, and obviously what
worries us the most is that where you have rave
parties and where you have drugs, you're bound
to (8) .... organised crime. We'd obviously
appreciate any new law which (9) .... us
more powers to (10) .... this problem.'

Now check your answers in the Coursebook.

5 Weak, weaken (CB page 56)

In the text 'Rave to the grave' in the Coursebook, you read that the loud music *weakened* the structure of the floor. Match the verbs 1–4 to the nouns a–d.

1. tighten
2. deepen
3. shorten
4. widen

a. your understanding
b. the waiting time
c. your belt
d. the gap

The verbs 1–4 in the left-hand column are common in newspaper headlines. Use them to complete these headlines.

5. Call to .... hospital waiting lists.
6. Gap between rich and poor set to ....
7. Government to .... immigration controls.
8. Economic fears ....

Now match the verbs 9–11 to the nouns e–g.

9. strengthen
10. loosen
11. lengthen

e. the time-scale
f. the relationship
g. the knot

Now complete these sentences with the verbs 9–11 above.

12. Russia wants to .... its ties with the West.
13. The days are beginning to .... again, thank goodness!
14. I think I've eaten too much. I'm going to .... my belt.

6 Expressions with *give*

In the conversation in the Coursebook, Steve said: 'I might give you a ring.' Complete the expressions in the sentences below with the words in the box.

advice	lift
answer	message
hand	priority
headache	regards

1. Bye. See you soon. Give my .... to your parents.
2. If you're going to work abroad, the best .... I can give you is to sort out your accommodation before you get there.
3. A: Sorry, Fiona's not here. She's just gone out.
   B: OK. Can you give her a(n) .... from me?
4. Is there any chance you could give me a(n) .... to the station?
5. I hope I'll be able to meet you, but I can't give you a definite .... until tomorrow.
6. I'm going. This music's too loud. It's giving me a(n) ....
7. Can I give you a(n) .... with your bags?
8. The problem with this company is we don't give .... to staff training.

7 Time and money

We spend time and we spend money. Complete the pairs of sentences below with the correct form of the words in the box.

can't afford	spare
run out of	spend
save	waste
short of	worth

1a. Do you .... much time surfing the internet?

1b. I .... too much on holiday. My credit card bill was enormous.

2a. I need to go to the bank. I've .... cash.

2b. I couldn't do everything I wanted to. I just .... time.

3a. I try to .... a little bit every month.

3b. Don't go by car. Take the train. It'll .... you a lot of time and a lot of hassle.

4a. That was the worst film I've ever seen. It was a complete .... of time.

4b. £25,000 for a car? What a(n) .... of money!

5a. My car cost £25,000 but it's probably only .... about £10,000 now.

5b. It's not .... going all the way to Scotland just for one day.

6a. After I've paid all my monthly bills, I've got no .... cash at all.

6b. What do you do in your .... time, then?

7a. I'd like to upgrade my computer, but I just .... to do it at the moment.

7b. I'd love to do an art course in the evenings, but I just .... the time at the moment.

8a. A: Steve, can I have a quick word with you?
   B: Yes, but I can't talk for long. I'm a bit .... time.

8b. A: So, are you going to come skiing with us at the weekend, then?
   B: I would if I could, but just at the moment I'm a bit .... cash.

Language note

A common saying in English is *time is money*. This is a metaphor. Many of the expressions in Exercise 7 contain language which is metaphorical: *spend time, save time, spare time, short of time,* etc. You can build your active vocabulary by learning the metaphorical uses of common words.

8 Verb + preposition

Make sentences by choosing the correct preposition and the best natural ending.

1. I agree

2. It depends

3. I worry   about

4. I'm waiting   for

5. I'm looking   of

6. He insisted   on

7. Don't blame me   with

8. That reminds me

a. { what happened. / something you did. / the mistake.

b. { everything you said. / you. / your idea in principle.

c. { something that happened last week. / a holiday I had in Wales once. / the time we lost our car keys.

d. { paying for himself. / having everything in writing. / punctuality at all times.

e. { a cheque to come through. / them to phone me back. / a fax.

f. { the future. / not having enough money. / my daughter.

g. { the weather. / how I'm feeling. / more than one thing.

h. { something more in life. / a new job. / the shoe department.

9 | Writing: a story

Write a story about the best or worst party you have ever been to, ending with the words: 'It was easily the best party I had ever been to' or 'It was easily the worst party I had ever been to'.

Sample story
Complete the first part of the story with the correct form of the verbs in the box.

call   catch up with   look forward to   miss

I'd really been (1) . . . . Alan's house warming party – 'Everyone will be there,' he had said. That meant it was a chance to (2) . . . . lots of friends, but it was also a chance for me to see Alan's sister again. I really liked her, but I hadn't had the courage to get her, phone number and (3) . . . . her. Seeing her at the party was an opportunity not to be (4) . . . .

Complete the second part of the story with the correct form of the verbs in the box.

get engaged   sense   sit around   warm up

I got there quite late, hoping the atmosphere would definitely have started (5) . . . ., but I (6) . . . . something wasn't quite right as soon as I walked in. There was no music and hardly any people. Alan took me into the dining room, where all his family were (7) . . . ., eating and chatting. Alan explained that he'd decided to turn the party into mostly a family occasion because – great news – his sister had just (8) . . . .! So, a house warming and engagement party combined!

Complete the last part of the story with the correct form of the verbs in the box.

die   insist   put on   spend

I then (9) . . . . the next two hours talking to members of Alan's family, looking at old photos, and eating Alan's grandmother's homemade sausage rolls. Alan's mother then (10) . . . . some music from the sixties that she (11) . . . . we all dance to. I nearly (12) . . . . of embarrassment. I left as soon as I could. It was easily the worst party I had ever been to.

Now write about the best or worst party you have ever been to. Think about these topics for your paragraphs:
- When was it? Whose party was it? Where was it?
- What kind of people were there and how did you feel when you arrived?
- What happened to make it so good/bad?
- How did you feel about it afterwards?

The language in the boxes below will help you. Check any words you don't know in your dictionary.

Atmosphere	Music	Food
brilliant	deafening	all home-made
dead	good to dance to	awful
electric	in the background	delicious
relaxed	lively	hardly any
tense	loud	lots of it
weird	slow	tasty

Other people	The party in general
All my friends were there.	It finished really early.
I didn't know anybody.	It never really got started.
I knew hardly anybody.	It took a while to warm up.
I met loads of new people.	It went on all night.

9 Last night

1 Collocations: *have, get* (CB page 65)

Complete the text below with the words and phrases in the box.

air	dinner
annoyed	home
argument	phone call
attacked	problems
back	shower
changed	something to eat
day	to bed

I had a terrible (1) . . . . yesterday. I had a few
(2) . . . . at work. First of all, I had a(n)
(3) . . . . with my boss about a small mistake
I'd made in a letter. I said sorry, but he just shouted at
me. He's impossible to work with.

At lunchtime I went out to get some fresh
(4) . . . . and had (5) . . . . in the
park. When I got (6) . . . . , I had a very
difficult (7) . . . . from a customer who was
still waiting for an order he sent in over a month ago.
He got quite (8) . . . . and asked to speak to
my boss.

Five o'clock finally arrived. As soon as I got
(9) . . . . , I had a(n) (10) . . . . and
got (11) . . . . I poured myself a drink and
then had (12) . . . . with my wife and
children. Later on, I went out for a walk and nearly
got (13) . . . . by a large dog. I was glad to get
(14) . . . . ! What a day!

Write the expressions with *have* and *get* in the correct column.

Have	Get

2 Had to (CB page 66)

**In the Coursebook, Lucy told Rose: 'I missed the
last train home and had to get a cab.' Look at
these patterns:**

I missed the last bus, and had to get a taxi.
I forgot to pack my shaving stuff, so I had to buy a new
razor.

**Make sentences by matching the beginnings 1–10
to the endings a–j.**

1. I ran out of cash, so I had to
2. I missed my train and had to
3. I didn't have any coffee in the flat, so I had to
4. I lost my passport and had to
5. I fell and sprained my ankle and had to
6. I almost ran out of petrol, so I had to
7. I felt really ill, so I had to
8. I spilled coffee all over my jeans, so I had to
9. I arrived about an hour late and had to
10. I realised I was on the wrong bus, so I had to

a. borrow some from my neighbours.
b. go home and get changed.
c. go down to the cash machine.
d. stop off at a garage. Sorry I'm late.
e. get off, go back, and wait for the right one.
f. go to the Embassy for a temporary one.
g. phone work and tell them I wouldn't be in.
h. wait three hours for the next one.
i. apologise to everyone.
j. go to hospital for an X-ray.

3 Managed to

If you managed to do something, you were able to do it, but with some difficulty. For example:

We couldn't get a seat with BA, but eventually we managed to find one on a KLM flight.

Complete the sentences below with the phrases in the box.

did you manage to get	managed to get tickets
managed to find	managed to park
managed to get	managed to persuade

1. It was murder trying to find a parking space, but I finally . . . . outside the flat.
2. You'll be pleased to know I . . . . for 'Phantom of the Opera' for next Friday.
3. I . . . . my parents to pay for driving lessons. My first one's next week.
4. It's been a struggle, but I've finally . . . . a few days off next week.
5. I've finally . . . . the holiday I've been looking for.
6. . . . . me a 'Times'?

4 Sleep and dreams (CB page 66)

In the conversation in the Coursebook, Rose says she fell asleep in the middle of a TV programme. Match the expressions 1–3 to the expressions with the opposite meaning a–c.

1. I'm a light sleeper.
2. I'm half asleep.
3. I slept like a log.

a. I didn't sleep a wink.
b. I'm a heavy sleeper.
c. I'm wide awake.

Now complete the short dialogues below with the expressions in the box.

it was an absolute nightmare	it went like a dream
it's like a dream come true	let's sleep on it

4. A: I hear your exam went very well.
   B: Yes, ...
5. A: Was your journey as awful as mine?
   B: You're not joking. . . . . !
6. A: I hear you've won a trip to South Africa!
   B: Yes, ...
7. A: So, are we going to make the decision today or not?
   B: . . . . and see what it feels like tomorrow morning.

5 Responding with auxiliaries (CB page 67)

Complete these short dialogues with the correct auxiliaries in the responses.

1. A: My father's just been on the phone.
   B: . . . . he? What . . . . he want?
2. A: I found someone's wallet in the street on the way to work this morning.
   B: . . . . you? . . . . you reported it to the police?
3. A: We've decided to trade in the Skoda for a Volvo.
   B: . . . . you? What model . . . . you getting?
4. A: I met Jennifer Lopez at the weekend.
   B: . . . . you? Where . . . . you meet her?
5. A: I've just had malaria.
   B: . . . . you? How . . . . you get it?
6. A: I'm going out with Helena tonight.
   B: . . . . you? How . . . . you manage that!
7. A: We're having my gran to dinner tonight.
   B: . . . . you? I . . . . know she lived near here. . . . . you see much of her?
8. A: I watched that awful thing last night about the famine in Ethiopia.
   B: . . . . you? I . . . . get home in time, but Jane recorded it on video for me.
9. A: I could let you borrow my camcorder for a few days, if you like.
   B: Oh, ... you? That . . . . be great!
10. A: We're considering moving out of town.
    B: . . . . you? . . . . you like life in town, then?
11. A: I was thinking of ringing my brother.
    B: . . . . you? Why . . . . you, then? He'll be really pleased if you . . . . What's the time in Sydney?
12. A: I feel my English is really improving.
    B: . . . . you? Why . . . . you think that?
    A: Well, I'm learning more useful expressions instead of just boring myself to death with the same old grammar points!

This exercise practised auxiliaries, but did you notice the expressions in the dialogues above? Complete them.

13. trade . . . . one car . . . . another
14. on the . . . . to work
15. go . . . . with someone you like
16. get home in . . . .
17. move . . . . of town
18. bore yourself to . . . .

6 I bet + auxiliary (CB page 67)

Complete the common expressions in these short dialogues with the correct auxiliaries.

1. A: I had a brilliant weekend in Copenhagen.
   B: I bet you . . . . ! I wish I'd gone myself.

2. A: I'm really annoyed about that ticket.
   B: I bet you . . . . ! You must be furious!

3. A: I've got a dreadful hangover this morning.
   B: I bet you . . . . ! You wouldn't stop when I told you you'd had too much!

4. A: I'll be so pleased when this course is over!
   B: I bet you . . . . ! Then you can take it easy for a bit.

5. A: It was so hot on the beach.
   B: I bet it . . . . ! I bet it was crowded too, wasn't it?

6. A: We were stuck on the motorway for three hours. It was awful.
   B: I bet it . . . . ! What a nightmare!

7. A: I can't wait to go on holiday next week.
   B: I bet you . . . . ! I wish I could go with you.

8. A: I really hate commuting every day.
   B: I bet you . . . . ! I would, too. It must be a real pain in the neck.

7 Until (CB page 66)

In the conversation in the Coursebook, Lucy said: 'I didn't get in until three!' Write six sentences using this pattern and the information in brackets. For example:

I usually leave work at six. (seven thirty)
I *didn't leave work until seven thirty.*

1. The class normally finishes at four. (half past four)
   It . . . .

2. The bank normally opens at nine. (quarter past nine)
   It . . . .

3. I started driving when I was eighteen. (thirty-five)
   I . . . .

4. We should have got home by midnight. (2 am)
   We . . . .

5. Most people get married in their twenties. (thirty-nine)
   John . . . .

6. A lot of people retire early these days. (seventy)
   My father . . . .

8 So/such (CB page 66)

Make phrases with *so* or *such*.

1. . . . . a good time
2. . . . . a lot of noise
3. . . . . a pity
4. . . . . a shock
5. . . . . a windy day
6. . . . . bad luck
7. . . . . cheap
8. . . . . disappointing
9. . . . . few people
10. . . . . fun
11. . . . . funny
12. . . . . interesting
13. . . . . many people
14. . . . . much money

Now complete these sentences with one of the expressions above.

15. It was . . . . that it was actually impossible to put the tent up.

16. Everything was . . . . that we bought as much as we could carry.

17. She's got . . . . ! She doesn't think twice about buying new clothes or jewellery.

18. It was . . . . to see my brother standing there. I thought he was still in Japan.

19. I went to one of those open air rock concerts for the first time last week. It was mad. There were . . . . and . . . . that I was actually a bit frightened at first.

Joke
A: Why are so many artists Italian?
B: I don't know.
A: Because they were born in Italy.

9 Writing: an awful experience (CB page 66)

In the conversation in the Coursebook, Lucy talked about her experience in an awful disco and her really late night. Write about a similar situation in your own life. Here are some ideas to help you.

When was it?
A couple of years ago …
When I was at college …

Who were you with?
a couple of friends
a group of us from work

How did the evening start?
We met up in a pub/bar/ outside the club.
We had a few drinks/had a bite to eat.

What happened next?
We decided to go on to …
We ended up going to …

What was it like?
It was awful.
It was full of teenagers/ people in their forties.

How did the evening finish?
We had to walk home/get a taxi.
I didn't get home until …

10 Relationships

1 He fancies you!

Complete the sentences below with the correct form of the verbs in the box.

ask out	fall	find	flirt
chat up	fancy	finish with	see

1. I tend to . . . . bald men quite attractive, actually.
2. You can't take Simon seriously. He . . . . in love with a different woman every week!
3. I think Caroline . . . . you. She's always . . . . with you – you must have noticed.
4. A: Is Michelle still . . . . Pete? They've been together for a few months, haven't they?
   B: No, actually, she . . . . him last week.
5. I want to . . . . Rachel . . . . for a drink, but do you know anywhere nice round here I can take her?
6. A: Have you seen Rob anywhere?
   B: Yeah, he's over there trying to . . . . that girl by the bar.

2 Vocabulary: prefixes (CB page 72)

In the text in the Coursebook, Jamie said: 'I tend to find them a bit immature.' Match the prefixes *un-*, *dis-*, *ir-* or *in-* to the adjectives in the box below.

attractive	honest	relevant	sane
bearable	imaginative	respectful	secure
formal	organised	responsible	

un-   . . . .
       . . . .
dis-   . . . .
       . . . .
ir-   . . . .
       . . . .
in-   . . . .
       . . . .

Now complete these sentences with the adjectives you formed above.

1. That was the worst club I have ever been to. The noise was . . . .
2. I find men with beards totally . . . .
3. Can't you think of something better to do than that? You're so . . . .
4. He never plans, never thinks ahead – he's so . . . .
5. He never tells the truth. He's completely . . . .
6. The way you spoke to that old lady was rude and . . . .
7. You can't let your daughter go out with a thirty-five-year-old man. She's only seventeen. That's completely . . . .
8. You can fall in love with anyone. It doesn't matter how old they are – age is . . . .
9. My boyfriend just needs a bit more confidence. He's a bit . . . .
10. A twenty-year-old man going out with an eighty-year-old woman – that's . . . .!
11. We're going to have a(n) . . . . wedding – just a few friends and family, that's all.

3 Expressions with *break* (CB page 72)

In the text in the Coursebook, Jamie didn't know whether to break the news of his new girlfriend to his parents. Which of these collocations with *break* is impossible?

a. break my concentration
b. break my heart
c. break my mind
d. break the habit
e. break the law
f. break the silence

Now complete these sentences with a collocation from above. Use the correct form of *break*.

1. I love my old Mini. It's the best car I've ever had. It would . . . . if anything happened to it.
2. If your car isn't insured, then you are . . . . If you get caught, you'll be in serious trouble.
3. Please don't talk to me at the moment. It's . . . . and I need to finish reading this before lunch.
4. I'm trying to stop biting my nails, but it's really difficult to . . . . I've been doing it as long as I can remember.
5. Everybody just sat there, saying nothing. Then Bob . . . . by blowing his nose and we all started laughing.

4 Phrasal verbs with *break*

Complete the sentences below with the words in the box.

> down (x3)   in   into   off   out (x2)   up (x2)

1. You'll never believe this. I'm at the side of the motorway. The car's broken . . . .
2. A: What time did the party finish? Late?
   B: Not really. It started to break . . . . around midnight.
3. Maria's broken . . . . her engagement to Paul. Apparently, she found out he wears a wig and likes Abba.
4. Fighting has broken . . . . again in Nepal.
5. I'm afraid someone broke . . . . last night and stole most of the computers.
6. When we heard the news of their deaths, most of us just broke . . . . What else could we do? They were so young.
7. Marriages can break . . . . or break . . . .
8. An epidemic of cholera has broken . . . . among the flood victims.
9. Someone broke . . . . the house when we were on holiday and made a terrible mess.

5 Expressions with *on* 1 (CB page 72)

In the text, you read that 'mixed marriages are on the increase'. Complete the sentences below with the expressions in the box.

> on business   on fire   on holiday   on strike
> on drugs   on foot   on line   on time

1. My flight's been cancelled. Apparently, the air traffic control people are . . . .
2. The buses here never arrive . . . . They're so unreliable. It drives me mad.
3. A: How did you get here? By car?
   B: . . . . , actually. I like a bit of exercise.
4. A: So, are you here on holiday?
   B: No, I'm . . . . actually.
5. I got back to my hotel to find it was . . . . and everybody was just standing in the street, watching the flames.
6. A: Where's Vince this week? Is he ill?
   B: No, he's . . . . He's gone to Brazil.
7. Brian and Gill are really worried that their son might be . . . . He's been acting really strangely lately.
8. I use the Internet mainly for chat rooms, where you can actually talk to people . . . .

6 Expressions with *on* 2

Complete the sentences below with the expressions in the box.

> on computer   on the map
> on the computer   on the motorway
> on the first floor   on the other line

1. Where on earth is Sacramento? See if you can find it . . . .
2. Hang on, I'll just check . . . .
3. The personnel department is . . . .
4. Can I speak to Mr O'Neil, please?
   I'm afraid he's . . . . Can I take a message or get him to phone you back?
5. What a journey! The traffic was awful and then we got a puncture . . . .
6. Did you know that the police have everybody's details . . . . , even if you have never committed a crime?

You *get on* a plane, a train and a bus, but you *get in* or *into* a car.

I got on the plane and went straight to my seat.
I got into the car and closed the door.

> ### Real English: *hang on*
>
> *Hang on* means *wait*.
> A: OK, are you ready?
> B: Hang on. I just need to get my bag.

7 Modal verb expressions (CB page 74)

Make sentences with modal verb expressions, as in the example.

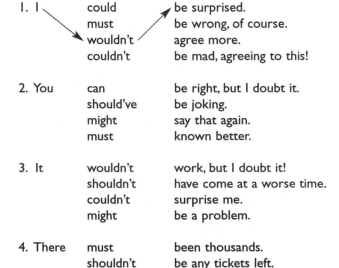

1. I
   - could
   - must
   - wouldn't
   - couldn't

   - be surprised.
   - be wrong, of course.
   - agree more.
   - be mad, agreeing to this!

2. You
   - can
   - should've
   - might
   - must

   - be right, but I doubt it.
   - be joking.
   - say that again.
   - known better.

3. It
   - wouldn't
   - shouldn't
   - couldn't
   - might

   - work, but I doubt it!
   - have come at a worse time.
   - surprise me.
   - be a problem.

4. There
   - must
   - shouldn't
   - can't
   - must've

   - been thousands.
   - be any tickets left.
   - be a mistake.
   - be any problem.

8 Won't

When things or people refuse to do what we want, we often use *won't* + verb. For example:

The car won't start. I'll have to call a taxi.

Complete the sentences below with *won't* and the words in the box.

> apologise   grow   help   lend   open   stop

1. I'm fed up with this weather. It just . . . . raining.

2. There's something wrong with the file on this CD. It . . . . What shall I do?

3. He knows he's upset me, but he still . . . .

4. Why . . . . you . . . . me? It'll only take a few minutes.

5. The bank . . . . me any more money. I'm not surprised really.

6. Plants just . . . . in my garden. I don't think I've got green fingers.

If you are talking about the past, just change *won't* to *wouldn't*. For example:

Sorry I'm late, the car wouldn't start.

9 *Can't have/must have + past participle*

Complete these sentences with *can't* or *must*.

1. A: I spent the whole day yesterday just cleaning the flat.
   B: That . . . . have been much fun.

2. A: You should've seen Neil doing his Madonna impression at the karaoke last night.
   B: That . . . . have been hilarious. I wish I'd been there.

3. A: I'm sorry to hear you were ill over the weekend. Are you OK now?
   B: Yes, I'm fine. I was just really sick for twenty-four hours. It . . . . have been something I ate.

4. A: You know, I'm sure I saw Debbie earlier in town.
   B: Well, it . . . . have been her. She's still in Canada. It might have been her sister. They're very similar-looking.

5. A: We're still waiting for Patrick to arrive. Do you think he's forgotten to come?
   B: He . . . . have forgotten. I only told him yesterday.

10 Writing: an e-mail

Sample e-mails
Read the two e-mails below, then complete Cathy's reply. Base your e-mail on the six questions in Judy's e-mail.

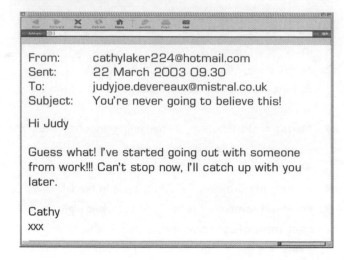

From: cathylaker224@hotmail.com
Sent: 22 March 2003 09.30
To: judyjoe.devereaux@mistral.co.uk
Subject: You're never going to believe this!

Hi Judy

Guess what! I've started going out with someone from work!!! Can't stop now, I'll catch up with you later.

Cathy
xxx

From: judyjoe.devereaux@mistral.co.uk
Sent: 22 March 2003 09.32
To: cathylaker224@hotmail.com
Subject: Re: You're never going to believe this!

Wow! When did this start? Who is he? What's he like? I bet he's gorgeous. Come on, do tell. Can you e-mail me a picture? When am I going to meet him (has he got any good-looking friends?)

I'm sitting here waiting for your reply!
Judy

From: cathylaker224@hotmail.com
Sent: 22 March 2003 10.45
To: judyjoe.devereaux@mistral.co.uk
Subject: Re: You're never going to believe this!

OK, OK, calm down. His name's . . . .
. . . .
. . . .
. . . .
. . . .
. . . .
. . . .
. . . .

11 Telling stories

1 Finish the story

Read this story and complete it using the words *drop*, *carry* and *stairs*.
Then compare what you have written with the answer key.

A man in Bristol is in hospital with burns and a broken leg after a bizarre incident in his bathroom last Saturday night. Apparently, the man woke up in the middle of the night, needing to go to the toilet. In the bathroom, he had a sudden craving for a cigarette, and so lit up while he was sitting on the toilet. A few minutes later, he dropped the cigarette down the toilet only to create a huge ball of fire, which shot out between the man's legs burning everything in its path. The noise of the explosion and the man's cries woke his wife, who immediately called an ambulance. The wife explained to the ambulance crew that before going to bed, she had taken her make-up off with an alcohol-based liquid and cotton wool, which she then threw into the toilet. It ignited when the cigarette was thrown in later that night.

That explains the man's burns but what about the broken leg? Apparently, the paramedics were laughing so much that they . . . . !

2 Adverbs 1

Complete the text below with the adverbs in the box.

accidentally fortunately instantly sadly suddenly surprisingly

An amazing coincidence

I was sitting on a bus quite happily in Amsterdam when a man got on and (1) . . . . sat on my hand. He said sorry and sat down.

Then I (2) . . . . realised the man was an uncle I hadn't seen for fifteen years. I recognised him (3) . . . . He hadn't changed at all. Not (4) . . . . , he was a bit shocked when I said, 'Hello Uncle Joe,' but (5) . . . . he recognised me and we quickly swapped telephone numbers and addresses.

I had to get off at the next stop, so we agreed to meet a few days later and we had a great time together. (6) . . . . , he was only there for a few more days, then he had to go back to Australia. We've kept in touch ever since.

3 Adverbs 2

Complete the sentences below with the adverbs in the box.

eventually luckily not surprisingly unfortunately

1. So, in the end, I got to the lecture really late.
   . . . . no one saw me arrive, so that was OK.
2. I'd promised Lisa I wouldn't be late, but the car wouldn't start. I arrived two hours late!
   . . . . , she was very annoyed.
3. We missed the last bus and had to walk all the way home. We . . . . got back about one in the morning.
4. We agreed we'd meet outside the bank, but . . . . he didn't realise which one I meant, so we didn't meet up in the end.

4 Adverbs 3

Complete the story of the shipwreck with the adverbs and adverbial expressions in the box.

amazingly	in the distance
later on	suddenly
the next thing we knew	to begin with
unfortunately	

We left Tangier late one Saturday night, heading for the Canary Isles. (1) . . . ., everything went well. Sunday was calm and the engine was running smoothly. By early evening the wind had got up. It was only force five or six – just normal for us. However, (2) . . . . that evening, the weather started to get worse. When morning came on the Monday, we were in the middle of one of the worst storms any of us had ever sailed in. Worse was to come.

It was about midday. (3) . . . ., without warning, the engine stopped. We sent out a mayday call on the radio, but there were no other ships in the area. We were on our own and we were terrified. (4) . . . . we could see a lighthouse. We knew the sea in that area was very dangerous and the wind was pushing us towards the land. (5) . . . ., a huge wave had thrown us onto the rocks beside the lighthouse. (6) . . . ., however, none of us was injured! The boat just sat there – high and dry! After an hour or two, when the tide had gone out, we used a ladder and climbed onto the rocks. Hundreds of people came to help us. My three shipmates and I were safe. (7) . . . ., we couldn't find Carlos, the ship's cat.

5 Shall I … or not? (CB page 76)

In the conversation in the Coursebook, Diane used the pattern *Shall I …?* twice. Match the situations 1–3 to the questions a–c.

1. You need a lift to the station. Your boss is about to leave. ☐

2. You're having a party. You've just got a new manager. You'd like to get to know him. ☐

3. You accidentally scratched your father's car when you borrowed it for the weekend. ☐

a. Shall I tell him or not?
b. Shall I invite him or not?
c. Shall I ask him or not?

Shall is often used with **we**. Now match the situations 4–8 to the suggestions d–h.

4. You've just found some love letters from your wife from the time before you married. ☐

5. Your son wants to have a party while you're on holiday. ☐

6. You're standing outside a Tunisian restaurant, wondering what it'll be like. ☐

7. You've just found a wallet with £50 in cash in it. ☐

8. Your neighbours are having a very noisy party. ☐

d. Shall we let him or not?
e. Shall we try it or not?
f. Shall we go round and complain or not?
g. Shall we keep it or not?
h. Shall we keep them or not?

Joke

Barman: I think you've had enough to drink now, sir. Shall I call you a taxi?
Drunk man: No, just call me Andy like everyone else does.

6 Have something done (CB page 76)

In the conversation in the Coursebook, Diane talked about the time she had her hair cut really short. When someone does something for you, you can use the structure *have something done*. For example:

I've just had the car fixed.
I've just had my video repaired.

Complete the sentences below with the correct form of the verbs in the box.

cut	pierce	re-design	take
install	redecorate	service	upgrade

1. A lot of people today have their ears, eyebrows, and noses . . . .

2. I don't like having my photograph . . . . I just get embarrassed.

3. It's about time I had my hair . . . . It's starting to look a bit of a mess.

4. We're having a new database system . . . . at work, which should make life a lot easier.

5. I can't e-mail you at the moment. I'm having my PC . . . . and I won't have it back till tomorrow.

6. I'm having my house . . . . at the moment, so it's in a bit of a mess.

7. I'll be a bit late in the morning. I'm taking my car in to have it . . . .

8. I'm thinking of having my back garden . . . . and that old shed removed.

7 -ing clauses (CB page 79)

Complete the sentences below with the words in the box.

finishing	thinking	watching
minding	waiting	wondering

1. I was just standing there, ... my own business.

2. I was just standing there, ... for the bus.

3. I was just standing there, ... the world go by.

4. I was just standing there, ... my cigarette.

5. I was just standing there, ... if anybody was going to serve me.

6. I was just standing there, ... : 'Shall I tell him or not?'

Match the places 7–12 to the sentences a–f.

7. in a shop ☐
8. stuck in a lift ☐
9. in a doctor's surgery ☐
10. at home ☐
11. in the car ☐
12. outside a friend's house ☐

a. So, anyway, I was sitting there, reading a magazine, trying not to worry too much.

b. So, anyway, I was standing there, waiting to be served.

c. So, anyway, I was sitting there, just watching TV.

d. So, anyway, I was driving along, listening to the radio.

e. So, anyway, I was standing there, trying not to panic, thinking: 'I hope someone comes soon.'

f. So, anyway, I was standing there, ringing the bell, wondering if I'd got the wrong day.

Make sentences by matching the beginnings 13–18 to the endings g–l.

13. He broke his arm ☐
14. She got her qualification ☐
15. He got malaria, ☐
16. She got arrested ☐
17. He made all his money ☐
18. She got married ☐

g. travelling through Kenya last July.
h. playing rugby.
i. thinking it would make her happy.
j. studying part-time at night school.
k. doing sixty miles an hour in the centre of town.
l. buying and selling property.

8 Train vocabulary

In the conversation in the Coursebook, Diane told the story about when she saw her dad on the underground (the tube). Complete the station announcement below with the words in the box.

buffet service	calling	change
coaches	platform	standing
travel		

Station announcement

The train now (1) . . . . at (2) . . . . three is the 7.33 to Cardiff, (3) . . . . at Southampton, Bournemouth, Bath and Bristol. Passengers for Bath should (4) . . . . in the front four (5) . . . . only. Passengers for Exeter should (6) . . . . at Bristol. Please note there is no (7) . . . . on this train.

Joke

Man:	A single to York, please.
Ticket clerk:	That's £13.75. Change at Leeds.
Man:	I want my change now – I'm not waiting till I get to Leeds!

Complete this conversation at the ticket office with the responses in the box.

£14.50
In about five minutes.
Number 4.
So you want a day return, that's £15.50.
That's an ordinary return, that's £22.60.
When are you coming back?

At the ticket office

A: How much is a single to Liverpool, please?

B: (8) ....

A: And a return?

B: (9) ....

A: Today.

B: (10) ....

A: What about if I come back tomorrow?

B: (11) ....

A: OK, just a day return then, please. What time's the next train?

B: (12) ....

A: And what platform is it?

B: (13) ....

A: Thanks.

9 Storytelling expressions

Complete the conversation below with the words and expressions in the box.

anyway	go on
guess what	lucky you
to cut a long story short	well
you're joking	

A: Did I tell you about what happened to me in Madrid last summer?

B: No, I don't think so – (1) ....

A: (2) ...., I was visiting the Madrid office for a couple of days, but I had some free time, so I decided to go the Reina Sofia gallery.

B: (3) ....!

A: Yes, well, (4) ...., I paid my money and got in the lift to go straight upstairs to the Picasso section, and (5) ....?

B: What?

A: The lift got stuck halfway and I was stuck there for two hours.

B: (6) ....! That's terrible. So, what happened?

A: Well, (7) ...., in the end they called the fire service to rescue me. I was more embarrassed than anything else. But they did give me my money back.

10 Vocabulary

Which of the expressions a–d are odd?

1. It was ... .
   a. a strange thing to happen.
   b. an odd thing to happen.
   c. a peculiar thing to happen.
   d. a happy thing to happen.

2. That was ... .
   a. a strange thing to say.
   b. a funny thing to say.
   c. a real thing to say.
   d. an unhelpful thing to say.

3. I couldn't believe my ... .
   a. eyes.
   b. mouth.
   c. luck.
   d. ears.

4. I'm dying ... .
   a. of a pain.
   b. to see my boyfriend.
   c. of hunger.
   d. for a drink.

5. I nearly died ... .
   a. of anger.
   b. laughing.
   c. when he told me.
   d. of embarrassment.

6. When my dad finally recognised me, he was ... .
   a. very embarrassed.
   b. quite embarrassed.
   c. a bit embarrassed.
   d. embarrassed some.

1 Cash and banks (CB page 83)

In the text in the Coursebook, you read about the twelve-year-old boy who went on a spending spree. Make compound words by matching the words 1–7 to the words a–g.

1.	credit	a.	machine
2.	exchange	b.	card
3.	local	c.	currency
4.	traveller's	d.	number
5.	bank	e.	account
6.	cash	f.	rate
7.	PIN	g.	cheques

Now complete this text with the compound words you formed above.

When I go abroad, I always take a small amount of cash in the (8) ...., just so I can buy things like snacks, bus tickets and so on as soon as I arrive. If I'm away for more than two days, I also take some (9) .... and cash them as and when I need more money.

If I buy anything expensive while I'm there, I use my (10) .... – it's so convenient and sometimes you get a better (11) .... You can also use it to withdraw money from a (12) ...., but I've never actually done that because I can never remember my (13) .... for that card. The year I worked in Finland I opened a Finnish (14) ....

Now complete these expressions with words from the text above.

15. a small/large .... of cash
16. .... a traveller's cheque
17. .... money from the cash machine/bank
18. .... /close a bank account

2 Money expressions

Complete the sentences below with the correct form of the verbs in the box.

cost	pick up	rip off	spend
splash out on	tighten	treat	watch

1. You can .... some real bargains at the market on Wednesdays.
2. We got .... by a taxi driver in Leeds. He charged us double what we should have paid.
3. I got paid on Friday and I went out on Saturday and .... myself to some new clothes.
4. I can't really afford it, but I think I might .... a new TV and DVD player.
5. You're not thinking of getting one of those flat screen TVs, are you? Those things .... an arm and a leg.
6. We spent too much this Christmas, so we're really going to have to .... our belts for a bit. At least till we've paid off the credit card bill.
7. I'm a bit worried about my mum. She's .... money like water at the moment. She's going to get into serious debt if she's not careful.
8. Money's a bit tight at the moment. I'm really having to .... what I spend.

3 I shouldn't have done that (CB page 83)

We all make mistakes. We often look back at our mistakes and say or think: 'I shouldn't have done that.'

Read this short story about two university students.

Two students at Oxford University were so confident of passing their end-of-year exams that instead of revising over the weekend they decided to go to a party.

On Monday morning they had terrible hangovers and were in no state to sit their exam. One of them phoned their professor and told him that they had gone away for the weekend and the car had broken down on the way back to Oxford, so they couldn't get there in time for the exam. The professor was very understanding. 'No problem,' he said. 'These things happen. You can take the exam on Wednesday.'

The students couldn't believe their luck. So on Wednesday the two students went in to the university to sit their exam, feeling very pleased with themselves. The professor put them into different rooms so they couldn't talk to each other and gave each of them the exam paper in a brown envelope. When they opened the envelopes, they found only one question to answer: 'Where exactly did the car break down?' Needless to say, they failed their exams!

Now complete these sentences with *should have* or *shouldn't have* and a past participle of a suitable verb.

1. The students . . . . the truth.
2. They . . . . a lie.
3. They . . . . at home and revised.
4. They . . . . to the party.
5. They . . . . more responsibly.

Real English: *needless to say*

This is said at the beginning of a sentence and means: *I don't need to say what I'm going to say because it is so obvious.*
The plane crashed in the Andes. Needless to say, there were no survivors.

4 Past simple and past continuous (CB page 84)

Complete this story with the correct form of the verbs in brackets.

Sorry I forgot about you!

A man from Nottingham now has the reputation for being the most insensitive husband in Britain. Brian Mills (1) . . . . (drive) into town with his wife when he suddenly (2) . . . . (realise) he (3) . . . . (need) to stop for petrol. While he (4) . . . . (fill up) the car, his wife (5) . . . . (go) into the petrol station to buy a magazine. Mr Mills (6) . . . . (finish) filling up the car, (7) . . . . (go) inside to pay, (8) . . . . (return) to the car and drove off.

Half an hour later he (9) . . . . (realise) his wife wasn't in the car with him, because when he (10) . . . . (offer) her a sweet, there was no reply.

He immediately (11) . . . . (drive) back to the petrol station where his wife (12) . . . . (wait) for him. 'It's not the first time Brian has done that,' she later (13) . . . . (tell) friends.

5 Pairs of verbs

Complete the sentences below with the pairs of verbs in the box.

arrived / rolling	got / brushing
came / leaving	had / waiting
didn't see / arguing	knocked / chasing
fell / trying	lost / shopping

1. The queen . . . . just as they were . . . . out the red carpet.
2. My dad . . . . a heart attack while he was . . . . for the plane.
3. I . . . . my camera while I was . . . . in the Grand Bazaar.
4. The sun . . . . out just as we were . . . . the beach.
5. They . . . . their little boy walk off while they were . . . . in the supermarket.
6. I . . . . a horrible pain while I was . . . . my teeth this morning.
7. The police . . . . someone down while they were . . . . a stolen BMW across town.
8. My watch . . . . to pieces while I was . . . . to put a new battery in.

6 | Conjunctions: *while, during, for*

Complete these sentences with *while, during* or *for.*

1. Can you look after my bag for a moment . . . . I pop into that shop? Thanks.
2. Where have you been? I've been waiting here . . . . ages.
3. I was quite self-conscious and shy . . . . my teenage years.
4. I was so tired last night I fell asleep . . . . I was watching TV. I felt terrible when I woke up.
5. I was so bored . . . . the talk, I slipped out for a coffee.
6. I won't be here on Monday. I'm going away . . . . a few days. I'll ring you on Thursday when I get back.

Now look at these examples with *just as* and *while*:

I got home just as the rain started.
Just as I was leaving the shop, a woman stopped me.
While I was waiting for the bus, I got talking to an old lady.
I finished reading the report while you were on the phone.

Complete these sentences with *just as* or *while*.

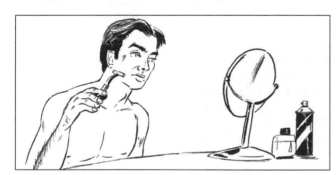

7. My bus arrived . . . . I was about to call a taxi.
8. I cut myself this morning . . . . I was shaving.
9. . . . . I finished the last question on the exam paper, the bell went.
10. There was a small earthquake . . . . I was in Turkey last month.
11. There was a loud bang . . . . we took off, but everything was all right.
12. Someone called for you . . . . you were at lunch, but they didn't leave their name.

7 | *Some* and *any*

***Some* means *not all*.**

I like jazz. (but not necessarily all)
I don't like some jazz. (but I like most jazz)

***Any* means *all* or *none*.**

I like any jazz. (all)
I don't like any jazz. (none at all)

All the other *some/any* words (*somebody, anybody, somewhere, anywhere*, etc.) are used in a similar way. Because of its meaning, *some* is more common in positive statements and *any* is more common in negative statements.

Write A (all), N (none) or NA (not all) next to these sentences, depending on the meaning of *some* and *any*.

1. I like any sport. . . . . .
2. I like some sports. . . . . .
3. I don't like any of those colours. . . . . .
4. I don't like some of those colours. . . . . .
5. Some people I knew were there. . . . . .
6. Anybody could tell you that! . . . . .

Now complete these sentences with *some*, *any*, or words formed from them.

7. He doesn't drink . . . . alcohol – not even wine.
8. I'll be in the office all day, so you can phone . . . . time between nine and five thirty.
9. I really enjoyed the film, but . . . . of my friends thought it was too slow.
10. I think there's . . . . at the door. Have a look. I'm sure I heard . . . .
11. Have you seen my keys? I can't find them . . . .
12. I don't know exactly where Trento is, but it's . . . . in the north-east of Italy.

Both *some* and *any* are correct and common in questions.

Can I get you something to eat?
Can I get you anything to eat?

The first question suggests the speaker has already thought about preparing some food or has something particular in mind. The second is a totally 'open' question.

> **Joke**
>
> Patient: Doctor, I need some advice. I seem to be getting fat in certain places. What can I do?
> Doctor: Simple! Stay away from those places.

8 Expressions with *take*

Complete the expressions in the sentences below with the words in the box.

advantage	risks
aspirins	size
coat	sugar
long	taxi
photo	time

1. Excuse me. Would you mind taking a(n) . . . . of me and my friends? You just press this button.
2. What . . . . shoes do you take?
3. A: Going by train would cost £25.60 return.
   B: And how . . . . does it take?
4. A: Tea or coffee?
   B: Coffee please.
   A: Do you take . . . . ?
5. A: Is your headache any better?
   B: Not yet, but I've just taken a couple of . . . . , so I should be OK in a while.
6. A: Right. I'm nearly ready. I just need to do a couple of things.
   B: There's no rush. Take your . . . .
7. A: We'll go by bus, shall we?
   B: I thought we'd take a(n) . . . . It'd be so much easier.
8. If you want to make money on the stock market, you've got to take a few . . . .
9. Hello, Mr Daniels, come in. Let me take your . . . .
10. We're going to take . . . . of the good weather and have a barbecue on the beach.

Go back and underline all the expressions with *take* above.

9 Vague language (CB page 86)

What do you think the missing numbers are in these sentences?

1. The journey only takes thirty or . . . . minutes.
2. There were only twenty or . . . . people in the whole cinema.
3. There must have been . . . . or five thousand people in the streets.
4. I'm nearly ready. I'll only be a minute or . . . .
5. I'll post it today and it should be with you in three or . . . . days.
6. I've had a word with . . . . or two people about your ideas.

Now complete these sentences with *something* or *anything*.

7. Pete was in a funny mood. He didn't say goodbye or . . . .
8. She said her name was Cathcott or . . . .
9. Shall we go out for a walk or . . . . ? I need some fresh air.
10. It's a fantastic restaurant and the bill only came to thirty- . . . . pounds for the three of us.
11. We were so busy we didn't have time to eat or . . . .
12. We don't know why the car went off the road. It could have been mud, water, or . . . . like oil on the road.

10 Writing: a naughty incident

Write about the naughtiest thing you did when you were younger. Here are some ideas to help you.

Paragraph 1
How old were you?
I must have been about eight …
I was in my early teens …
Where were you?
I was all alone in the house …
I was out with some friends …
What happened?
I decided to …
I thought it would be a laugh to …

Paragraph 2
Did anyone find out? If so, how, and how did they react?
When my mum came in …
My parents went ballistic!
Nobody ever found out.

Paragraph 3
How do you feel about it now?
Looking back, it was quite funny.
Looking back, it could've been really serious. I mean, just imagine if …
Looking back, I must've been mad.
I still feel a bit bad about it.

13 Old friends

1 Past simple and present perfect

Read these texts about three football heroes and choose the correct alternative.

Pele

Pele was perhaps the best footballer the world (1) *ever saw / has ever seen*. He (2) *played / has played* ninety-two times for Brazil and (3) *scored / has scored* seventy-two goals. He was strong, fast, and very skilful. He (4) *won / has won* the World Cup with Brazil three times: in 1958, 1962 and 1970. He (5) *scored / has scored* in the 1970 final, and Brazil beat Italy 4–1. It was because of Pele and that wonderful Brazilian team that people (6) *started / have started* calling football 'the beautiful game'.

David Beckham

The superstar of English football is David Beckham. He (7) *joined / has joined* Manchester United as a schoolboy and so far (8) *made / has made* over 300 appearances for the club. He (9) *played / has played* forty times for England. He (10) *became / has become* famous around the world when he (11) *was / has been* sent off for kicking an Argentinean, Diego Simeone, in the 1998 World Cup. A year later, he (12) *married / has married* Victoria Adams, one of the Spice Girls. He (13) *won / has won* nearly everything a player can win – except the World Cup.

Morgan Lewis

Born in the sixties, Lewis (14) *played / has played* for all his school teams and (15) *represented / has represented* the south-west of England schoolboy team. At the age of eighteen, he (16) *signed / has signed* as a professional for AFC Bournemouth in the second division, choosing to play for his home town team instead of Manchester United, Juventus or Real Madrid.

During his short career, Lewis (17) *suffered / has suffered* several bad injuries and (18) *only played / has only played* fifteen times for the Bournemouth first team. In his final year with the club at the age of twenty-one, Bournemouth (19) *won / has won* the second division championship. Injury (20) *ended / has ended* his playing days soon after that. His mother still says that he is the best player she (21) *ever saw / has ever seen* – and that includes Pele and David Beckham!

2 Present perfect simple and present perfect continuous (CB page 94)

Choose the more probable alternative in these sentences.

1. *Have you seen / Have you been seeing* my mobile phone anywhere? I think I've lost it.
2. *Have you seen / Have you been seeing* another woman behind my back?
3. Have you been away or something? *I've tried / I've been trying* to ring you all week.
4. A: If you want to stop smoking, why don't you try those nicotine patches that you put on your arm? They might help.

   B: *I've tried / I've been trying* those before and they don't work.
5. I feel a lot better since *I've taken / I've been taking* extra vitamins.
6. *It's taken / It's been taking* me fifteen years to get to this position in the company. You have to be ambitious and patient in this job.
7. What a stink! Someone *has smoked / has been smoking* in here. Open the window!
8. Sorry I'm late. *Have you waited / Have you been waiting* long?

3 For/since

Complete these sentences with *for* or *since*.

1. I've been working here .... as long as I can remember.
2. I've been working here .... the mid-nineties.
3. He's been on the phone .... ages.
4. It's been years .... I had a holiday.
5. I've only been here .... a couple of minutes. I got here just before you.
6. I've been a bit depressed .... I lost my job.
7. I've been feeling ill .... the last couple of days. I think it's flu.
8. My family moved to Sydney when I was only four and I've lived here ever ....
9. My family's lived in this house .... 1927.
10. I've been married .... seven years.

When you want to stress the length of time, use *ever since*. For example:

We've lived in the same house ever since we got married.
I've steered clear of Julia – ever since I heard that all four of her husbands died in the bath.

> **Famous present perfect**
> 'I've tried being rich and I've tried being poor; rich is better.' (Mae West, actress)

4 | Expressions with *for*

For is used in many different expressions. Complete the sentences below with the expressions in the box. Then think how you would say the same expressions in your own language.

for Christmas	for lunch	for next Monday
for her age	for more details	for sale

1. My dad bought me a watch . . . .

2. I see that house at the end of the street is . . . . I wonder how much they want for it.

3. My mum's sixty-eight, but she's very fit . . . .

4. It's nearly one o'clock – time . . . .

5. I've made an appointment . . . . at two o'clock. Is that OK?

6. Contact us now on 0800 778 675 . . . .

Now complete the sentences below with the expressions in the box.

famous for	late for	responsible for
good for	ready for	sorry for

7. Right, I'd better go – otherwise I'm going to be . . . . my appointment.

8. Pamplona's . . . . bull-running.

9. You've got to be . . . . anything in this job.

10. I feel . . . . those people begging in the underground. They've got a terrible life.

11. I'm . . . . sales and marketing in Eastern Europe.

12. It says in the newspaper here that wine is actually . . . . you. Is that true?

Answer these questions.

13. Is wine good for you?
14. What's your town famous for?
15. Do you feel sorry for people who have to beg?
16. What are you responsible for in your job?

5 | Ending a conversation (CB page 94)

In the Coursebook Barry said: 'I'd best be off' when he wanted to finish the conversation. Make expressions for ending conversations by putting the words in the right order. Begin as shown.

1. Well, / must / really / I / going / be
    Well, ...

2. Well, / nice / it / talking / was / to / you
    Well, ...

3. Right, / better / I'd / going / be
    Right, ...

4. Right, / time / I / was / it's / going
    Right, ...

5. Well, / nice / you / to / see / it's / again
    Well, ...

> **Real English: *Cheers!***
> You probably know that British people say *Cheers!* when they have a drink together. But *Cheers* can also mean *Bye* and *Thanks*.
> A: *Can I have a quick look at your newspaper?*
> B: *Sure, here you are.*
> A: *Cheers. (= Thanks.)*
>
> A: *Right. I'm off. See you tomorrow.*
> B: *Cheers, then. (= Bye.)*

6 | *It's time* + past simple

Did you notice the use of the past continuous with a present meaning in number 4 in Exercise 5 above: *It's time I was going*?

Re-write these sentences using *It's time* + past simple. For example:

I really need to get myself a mobile phone.
It's time I got myself a mobile phone.

1. I really should start my homework.
    It's time I . . . .

2. You've got to decide what you really want to do with your life.
    It's time you . . . .

3. Sooner or later, I really should learn how to drive.
    It's time I . . . .

4. My whole flat needs a good clean.
   It's time I . . . .

5. When is the government going to do something about old age pensions?
   It's time the government . . . .

6. I haven't been to the dentist for a check-up for ages.
   It's time I . . . .

7. I can't use my bike because I still haven't got it fixed.
   It's time I . . . .

7 Still, yet, already (CB page 94)

Complete these sentences with _still_, _yet_ or _already_.

1. I haven't sent off the forms . . . .
2. I've . . . . sent the forms off.
3. Have you . . . . got that old typewriter?
4. Can you believe I . . . . haven't decided where to go on holiday this year?
5. Haven't you read that book I lent you . . . . ?
6. A: Do you want to come and see that new Spielberg film?
   B: I've . . . . seen it, actually, so, sorry.
7. A: Do you like the new Robbie Williams CD?
   B: I haven't actually heard it . . . . Is it any good?
8. A: Have you heard the Robbie Williams CD . . . . ?
   B: No, I . . . . haven't heard it.

Notice these two meanings of _still_:

a. I still live with my parents. (still = up to now)
b. The weather was pretty bad, but we still had a good time. (still = in spite of that)

Which of these sentences are like a and which like b above?

9. We still can't get used to the idea she's gone. . . . . .
10. Despite the recession, we still made a good profit. . . . . .
11. I'm still waiting for an apology. . . . . .
12. There's still time to send in your application form. . . . . .
13. I missed my usual bus, but I still got to work on time. . . . . .

Re-write these sentences adding _still_ in the natural position.

14. We haven't heard a thing from the insurance company.
    . . . .
15. Are you working for IBM?
    . . . .
16. Are you annoyed with me?
    . . . .
17. Hurry up! We've got to get our tickets.
    . . . .
18. It's raining.
    . . . .
19. The post hasn't arrived.
    . . . .
20. In spite of all your arguments, I think you're wrong.
    . . . .
21. What needs to be done?
    . . . .

8 I wish (CB page 97)

Complete the text below with the correct form of the verbs in the box. One of them will be negative.

bother	keep in touch with	listen
realise	spend	tell

If I could turn the clock back, there are quite a few things I would change in my life. The first thing is, I wish I (1) . . . . to my parents more. I ignored most of their advice and so had to learn everything the hard way. I also wish I (2) . . . . going to university – it was a total waste of time. It didn't help me get a better job even though I worked really hard and got a good degree. To be honest, I wish I (3) . . . . more time partying and having a good time – at least then I would have enjoyed myself. I also wish I (4) . . . . some of my old school friends. I'd love to find out what they're up to now. I wish I (5) . . . . at a younger age that life is what you make of it, instead of waiting for it all to just happen. I wish someone (6) . . . . me that. Mind you, I probably wouldn't have listened. I thought I knew it all.

Notice that _I wish_ is often followed by the past perfect. Do you know these other common structures following _I wish_?

I wish I could sing.
I wish you would keep quiet.
I wish I lived in the city.
I wish I didn't have to commute every day.

14 Art

1 Expressing disapproval

Make expressions used by people at a modern art exhibition by putting the words in the correct order.

1. that / is / what / be / supposed / to / ?

....

2. laugh / having / are / they / a / ?

....

3. my / five-year-old / better / than / could / do / that

....

4. art / call / you / that / !

....

5. it / sense / any / doesn't / make / at / all / !

....

6. ridiculous / I've / ever / that's / seen / the / most / thing / !

....

2 Not recommending something
(CB page 99)

Complete the responses in these short dialogues by matching the beginnings in 1–4 to the endings a–d.

1. A: What was that art exhibition like?
   B: I'd give it a miss if I were you. ☐

2. A: What's that new Chinese restaurant like?
   B: I wouldn't bother if I were you. ☐

3. A: What's that new bar like opposite the Town Hall?
   B: I'd give it a miss if I were you. ☐

4. A: What's that new Spielberg film like?
   B: I wouldn't bother if I were you. ☐

a. The prices are ridiculous!
b. It was so boring, the plot was non-existent.
c. There was a fight the night I went.
d. It was mostly just ceramics, no paintings at all.

3 Collocations: *cause* (CB page 101)

Complete the sentences below with the words in the box.

accidents	damage	riot
chaos	outrage	sensation

1. Kylie Minogue caused a(n) .... last night with a dress that helped her to show off her best assets. Her arrival at the Pop Awards ceremony almost caused a(n) .... as hundreds of fans pushed forward to catch a glimpse of the star.

2. A small typhoon in West Sussex, England, has caused thousands of pounds worth of .... to houses in two villages.

3. A new report reveals that .... caused by people falling asleep while driving have increased by 10% over the last five years.

4. More heavy snow has caused .... on the roads with many motorways closed or only operating two lanes.

5. The latest Turner Prize winner has caused .... in the art world by producing an exhibition made up completely of sheep's eyeballs.

4 Adding a comment (CB page 102)

Make sentences by matching the beginnings 1–7 to the endings a–g.

1. There'd been an accident with a lorry, ☐
2. The weather suddenly turned cold, ☐
3. They wouldn't accept my credit card, ☐
4. There was a train strike, ☐
5. Then Pam arrived, ☐
6. And of course I don't speak Chinese, ☐
7. The whole class passed except me, ☐

a. which meant we had to cancel the trip.
b. which meant one lane of the motorway was closed.
c. which meant I was the only one who had to do it again.
d. which meant we had to stop talking about her!
e. which meant I couldn't explain what I wanted.
f. which meant I had to pay cash.
g. which meant we nearly froze to death on the beach.

5 Believe it or not

Put these comment clauses A–D in the correct place in the article below.

> **A.** which meant he was bound to lose the match
> **B.** which were very expensive
> **C.** which was now at the bottom of the lake
> **D.** which was only about a metre deep

A golfer playing in a club competition was playing so badly that he really lost his cool. When he took twelve shots at the fifteenth hole, [1] , he picked up his golf bag and threw it into the nearby lake, [2] , and stormed off to the clubhouse. Nobody was surprised when, two minutes later, the man returned to get his clubs, [3] .
He took off his shoes, rolled up his trousers and went into the water to find the bag, [4] . When he found it, however, he just took his car keys out of it, and threw the bag back into the water.

6 Adjective + preposition

Match the adjectives 1–4 to the prepositions a–d.

1. typical   a. at
2. good   b. to
3. responsible   c. of
4. relevant   d. for

Now complete these sentences with the phrases you formed above.

5. I'm quite . . . . tennis.
6. I agree with what you're saying, but it's not really . . . . the discussion.
7. I'm . . . . five people in my department.
8. I'm not surprised the train was delayed. That's . . . . our train service.

Which adjective + preposition from above goes with these words?

9. That's . . . .
              him.
              this government.
              British cars.

Match the adjectives 10–13 to the prepositions e–h.

10. aware   e. for
11. satisfied   f. of
12. suitable   g. to
13. similar   h. with

Now complete these sentences with the phrases you formed.

14. In my opinion, a lot of children's TV is not really . . . . children at all.
15. I like the colour of that car. It's quite . . . . one I had a few years ago.
16. I bought a Mazda last year and I'm very . . . . it. I've had no problems at all.
17. I don't think any of my friends take drugs. If they do, I'm certainly not . . . . it.

Which adjective + preposition from above goes with these words?

18. . . . .
          a problem
          the situation
          somebody looking at me

19. . . . .
          mine
          one I've seen before
          last year's model

20. . . . .
          the situation
          my job
          the service in the hotel

21. . . . .
          all ages
          the beach
          both men and women

7 | *The* or no *the*

In London, there are two art galleries with very similar names: The Tate and Tate Modern. There is no rule to explain why *the* is not used before Tate Modern. For places and organisations, you just need to remember whether they have *the* or not.

Complete these sentences with *the* where necessary. Only five sentences need *the*.

1. An uncle of mine works for .... Bank of England.

2. Have you ever been to .... National Gallery in London?

3. This time last week, I was actually walking along .... Fifth Avenue in New York.

4. Have you ever been to .... America?

5. Have you ever been to .... United States?

6. Does the President actually live in .... White House?

7. Does the Queen actually live in .... Buckingham Palace?

8. Why doesn't Switzerland want to be part of .... European Union?

9. My dad, my brother and both my sisters all work for .... Sony. Amazing, isn't it?

Language note

Notice which of the following take the definite article *the*:

The Kremlin	Buckingham Palace
The Vatican	Disneyland
The Louvre	American Express
The Amazon	Loch Ness
The Eiger	Mount Everest
The BBC	CNN
The Titanic (the ship)	'Titanic' (the film)
The First World War	Harrods

Here are some examples which show the difference very clearly:

Have you seen 'Death on the Nile'?
The death was reported in all the papers.

Buckingham Palace is a very large place for two people and a few dogs.
A spokesman for the Palace said the Queen was very tired after her long trip.

Mercedes are worried about losing sales in the US.
The Mercedes is still one of the classiest cars around.

The Titanic was one of the most famous ships.
'Titanic' is one of the most famous films ever made.

8 | Remind, remember (CB page 102)

On page 102 of the Coursebook, you practised 'That reminds me.' Complete these sentences with *remind* or *remember*.

1. That shop assistant really .... me of your brother. They've got the same eyes.

2. A: Don't forget to get a birthday card for Fiona, will you?
   B: I won't have time today. Can you .... me about it tomorrow, otherwise I'll forget?

3. Can I .... you to look at that report I gave you last week? I need some feedback by Monday.

4. A: Do you .... that time when you got to the airport and found you'd left your passport at home?
   B: Don't .... me! I still have nightmares about it.

5. A: I've just been to the library, but it was closed.
   B: Oh, that .... me, I've got to take a book back. Why was it closed?

6. Bye. Have a good time in Scotland. .... me to your parents.

Many of the expressions above are very common. First check your answers in the answer key, then complete these expressions with *remind* or *remember*.

7. (He) .... me of (your brother).
8. .... me to (your parents).
9. Can I .... you to (ring the bank)?
10. Do you .... the time (we got lost)?
11. That .... me. (When do we leave?)
12. Can you .... me about it, please?
13. You .... me of someone I know.

Here are two more expressions. Complete them with *remind* or *remember*.

14. If I .... rightly, (the talk starts at ten).
15. My aunt .... me in her will. (She left me £10,000.)

Can you think of another common way of saying: 'Remember me to your wife'?

9 I keep meaning to ...

Complete the responses in these short dialogues by matching the beginnings in 1–6 to the endings a–f.

1. A: I got a call from Susie this morning.
    B: Did you? I keep meaning to ☐

2. A: Have you got time to see my holiday photos?
    B: Yes, OK. That reminds me, I keep meaning to ☐

3. A: Do you fancy a game of squash tomorrow night?
    B: Yes, great. Can I borrow your spare racket again? I keep meaning to ☐

4. A: I've just been in that new sports shop. It's really good.
    B: Is it? I keep meaning to ☐

5. A: I'm leaving a bit early today – I've got the dentist at five.
    B: No worries. I keep meaning to ☐

6. A: I saw 'Gangs of New York' last night.
    B: Did you? I keep meaning to ☐

a. make an appointment myself. I haven't had a check-up for over a year.

b. buy one, but I just haven't had a chance.

c. speak to her myself. How is she?

d. go in and have a look around myself.

e. go and see it myself. Is it any good?

f. get a film developed, but I just keep forgetting.

10 Writing: an article

You have recently visited an art or photographic exhibition and your English teacher has asked you to write an article about it for the school magazine. Describe what you saw, give your opinion of the exhibition, and say whether you recommend it or not. Before you write your own article, do the task below.

Sample article
Put these sentences A–C in the correct place in the article.

> **A.** Quite the opposite, I'm afraid.
>
> **B.** That kind of thing just doesn't happen, does it?
>
> **C.** The first thing you see as you enter the exhibition is about a hundred filled plastic rubbish sacks all piled on top of each other.

You call that art?

Have you ever gone to the theatre but when inside, instead of seeing a play, you found it was a film? ☐ **1** Well, something like that happened to me last week when I visited the new 'Life in the City' art exhibition at the Civic Arts Centre. I don't really know what I saw there, but it wasn't art.

☐ **2** You are then treated to various 'urban realities', such as crushed coke cans in a puddle, bags of discarded fish and chips, a rusty bike that was chained to some railings, and a man (not a real one) asleep on the pavement in a sleeping bag. Most of the things I saw I could create myself – they take no artistic talent at all.

Call me traditional, but I was hoping for at least a few pieces of art that would make me say 'Wow' or leave me with admiration for the talents of the artists. ☐ **3** Unless you enjoy walking around things you could make yourself with a few bags and some old food, I recommend you stay at home with a good book.

Now write your own article for the school magazine. It can be positive, negative like the one above, or something in between.

Think of an interesting title, and try to catch the reader's interest with your opening sentence. Write three or four paragraphs, each with a purpose. Think about the following as you plan:

*   What was the exhibition and why did you decide to go and see it?

*   What were the exhibits like and who created them?

*   What were your reactions to some individual exhibits?

*   What were your reactions to the exhibition as a whole?

15 Describing things

1 Taste, smell, feel

Which adjectives go with the verbs *taste*, *smell* and *feel*? Put the words in the box below in the correct group. Sometimes a word goes in more than one group.

bitter	disgusting	off	sour
bland	fresh	sharp	spicy
cold	hard	smooth	sweet
delicious	horrible	soft	wet

It tastes: ....

....

It smells: ....

....

It feels: ....

....

Now complete these sentences with *taste, smell* or *feel* and an adjective from above.

1. Silk ....
2. Lemons ....
3. Indian food ....
4. This coffee ....
5. I can .... freshly-baked bread.
6. This milk .... Don't drink it.

> **Real English:** *this milk's off*
>
> If milk or cheese or meat is *off*, it means that it is too old to eat safely.

2 Opposites

Do you know the opposites? Guess before checking in the answer key.

1. mild cheese .... cheese
2. sweet white wine .... white wine
3. a hot curry a .... curry
4. a heavy meal a .... meal
5. milk chocolate .... chocolate
6. cooked fish .... fish
7. frozen vegetables .... vegetables
8. a well-done steak a .... steak
9. still mineral water .... mineral water

Now answer these questions.

10. Do you prefer mild cheese or strong cheese?
11. What about wine – sweet or dry?
12. Do you prefer milk or plain/dark chocolate?
13. Do you eat raw fish?
14. How do you like steak: rare, medium or well-done?

3 Collocations

Strong, weak
Complete these sentences with *strong* or *weak*.

1. I like things with lots of taste; you know, really .... coffee and .... cheese.
2. I can hardly understand Gustav. He's got such a .... accent.
3. My mother likes really .... tea. The way she likes it is almost like drinking water!
4. I'm going to be in York at the weekend myself, so there's a .... possibility we might bump into each other.
5. No wonder the company closed down! Their management was very ....
6. What this government needs is a .... leader.

Strong, firm, slight, mild
Complete these sentences with *strong, firm, slight* or *mild*.

7. Sarah speaks French with a very .... German accent. You hardly notice it.
8. Everything in the Canaries seemed very cheap because of the .... pound.
9. I'm a .... believer in being completely honest with people.
10. What I need is a cup of .... black coffee.
11. I'm not sure if I'm free at the weekend. There's a .... possibility my sister's coming to visit.
12. I prefer .... cheese. I really don't like the really strong kinds.
13. Do you mind if I don't come with you? I've got a .... headache.
14. Martina is now the .... favourite to win the tournament.

Now put the nouns from this exercise into the correct group. Then check your answers in the answer key.

Strong:	. . . .
Mild:	. . . .
Firm:	. . . .
Slight:	. . . .
Weak:	. . . .

4 Linked questions (CB page 105)

Match the questions 1–8 to the linked questions a–h.

1. How was the exam?
2. What was his girlfriend like?
3. What was it like on the beach?
4. How was your dinner party?
5. How was your dad?
6. Where are you going?
7. Who are you going to invite?
8. What was the weather like?

a. Were you able to ski?
b. Do you think you passed?
c. Was she nice?
d. Did everything go OK?
e. Anywhere special?
f. Was he OK?
g. Was it crowded?
h. Anyone I know?

Here are three responses. Match them to the correct questions above.

i. I'm not sure. I'll just have to wait and see.
ii. Just to that Italian restaurant on the corner.
iii. Yes, fine. Everybody seemed to enjoy themselves.

Two *must've* jokes

Dad:	Do you think our son got his intelligence from me?
Mum:	He must've done. I've still got mine.

Customer:	Waiter! This lobster only has one claw.
Waiter:	Sorry sir, it must've been in a fight.
Customer:	Well, bring me the winner, then.

5 Considering, although (CB page 105)

Make sentences by matching the beginnings 1–8 to the endings a–h.

1. It was really warm in Switzerland,
2. It's still a great car,
3. She doesn't get paid much,
4. The traffic wasn't too bad,
5. I'm not surprised how tired you are,
6. We had a great holiday,
7. I think CDs are too expensive,
8. I'm surprised you don't get a laptop,

a. considering they only cost about 50p to produce.
b. considering the time of year.
c. considering it was the rush hour.
d. considering it's done over eighty thousand miles.
e. considering what time you went to bed last night.
f. considering the hours she works.
g. considering how cheap they are now.
h. considering the whole country was on strike!

Now make sentences by matching the beginnings 9–14 to the endings i–n.

9. It's a great car. I really love it,
10. It was really warm in Switzerland,
11. The traffic wasn't too bad,
12. We had a great holiday,
13. I think CDs are too expensive,
14. I'm surprised you don't get a laptop,

i. although most people don't seem to mind.
j. although I don't suppose you work from home.
k. although it's a bit expensive on the petrol.
l. although I'm glad to be back home.
m. although it was a bit slow just outside London.
n. although it turned a bit cold at night.

Considering means *when you remember that or when you take into consideration that.* The comment after *although* contrasts with the meaning of the first part of the sentence.

6 In spite of

Complete the sentences below with the expressions in the box.

> in spite of her parents' opposition
> in spite of his injury
> in spite of his professional success
> in spite of the cost
> in spite of the snow
> in spite of their promises

1. Matthew is not actually a very happy person, ...
. . . .

2. We've decided to buy a brand new car, instead of a second-hand one, ...

3. They're still going to get married, ...
. . . .

4. . . . . , Miguel Indurain still intends to ride in the Alps.

5. We managed to get back to Paris by midnight, ...
. . . .

6. The Government has raised income tax twice, ...
. . . . !

Notice that we often use *in spite of the fact that* + *clause*. For example:

I went with them to the Indian restaurant in spite of the fact that I don't like curries.

7 ... , though

Look at this example:

I think Shakespeare's plays are amazing. They're not easy to read, though.

***Though* follows a comment which contrasts with what has just been said. It is very common at the end of a sentence in spoken English. Match the statements 1–8 to the comments a–h.**

1. I think India is the best place I've visited. ☐
2. I always buy two Sunday newspapers. ☐
3. Bungee jumping looks amazing, doesn't it? ☐
4. I don't go to church. ☐
5. I love decorating. ☐
6. I'm a vegetarian. ☐
7. I don't do any sport. ☐
8. It's not the best film I've ever seen. ☐

a. I couldn't do it myself, though.
b. I couldn't live there, though.
c. I do believe in God, though.
d. I don't always read them, though.
e. I'm glad I've seen it, though.
f. I don't get much chance to do it, though.
g. I do eat fish, though.
h. I think I'm quite fit, though.

8 Negative questions (CB page 107)

Complete the short dialogues below with the negative questions in the box.

> Haven't you heard?   Don't you like it?
> Didn't you get it?   Aren't you coming?

1. A: Have a good time at Tim's barbecue.
   B: . . . . ? I thought we were all going.
   A: No, I'm already doing something.

2. A: I'm still waiting for that fax I asked you for.
   B: . . . . ? I sent it as soon as I put the phone down yesterday.

3. A: I haven't seen Mark for ages. Is he OK?
   B: . . . . ? He's got a job in Canada.

4. A: Your tie's a bit bright. Is it new?
   B: . . . . ? It was a birthday present.

Now complete the short dialogues below with the negative questions in the box.

> Don't you remember?   Haven't you seen it?
> Didn't anyone tell you?   Wasn't it open?

5. A: I didn't know there was a meeting today.
   B: . . . . ? Sorry about that.

6. A: I couldn't get a newspaper. The shop was still closed.
   B: . . . . ? It's usually open at eight.

7. What's that new Kevin Spacey film like?
   B: . . . . ? It's brilliant. You must go.

8. Have you finished with that book I lent you?
   B: I gave it back to you ages ago.
   . . . . ? I brought it round to your house.

9 Expressions with *way* (CB page 106)

In the conversation in the Coursebook, Paul said: 'There was this guy sitting next to us who snored all the way through the film.' Complete the sentences below with the expressions in the box.

by the way	no way
change his ways	out of your way
either way	the other way round

1. A: So, we'll go to the beach in the morning and play tennis in the afternoon.
   B: I'd prefer it . . . . myself.
2. A: So, what do you want to do – have lunch here or shall we find somewhere else?
   B: I don't mind . . . . You decide.
3. A: Right, I'm off. See you tomorrow.
   B: OK. Oh, ... , are you still coming to lunch on Saturday?
4. A: Shall we meet at about four? Is that OK?
   B: There's . . . . I'll be ready by four. The earliest I can make it is five.
5. My dad pays cash for everything. I've tried to persuade him to use a credit card, but he says he's too old to . . . .
6. A: You don't need to get a taxi. I'll give you a lift.
   B: Well, OK, if it's not . . . .

10 Easily the biggest

What are they talking about? Match the descriptions 1–10 to the topics a–j.

1. It's got easily the fastest processor. ☐
2. It's got easily the best sound. ☐
3. It's easily the most environmentally friendly. ☐
4. It's got by far the best lens. ☐
5. It's by far the quickest route. ☐
6. It's by far the best one they've done so far. ☐
7. It's easily the scariest. ☐
8. It's by far the worst in living memory. ☐
9. It's got by far the best atmosphere in town. ☐
10. It's got easily the best selection. ☐

a. a hi-fi system
b. an earthquake
c. a computer
d. a horror film
e. a camera
f. a CD of a band
g. a new club
h. Virgin records
i. a car
j. a journey

11 Comparison

Look at this example:

The curry was hot – much hotter than I'd expected.

Complete these sentences as in the example.

1. It was an interesting film – . . . . than the reviews said it was.
2. It was quite funny – . . . . than I'd expected.
3. The journey was easy – . . . . than you said it would be.
4. The traffic was very bad – . . . . than usual.
5. It was a really comfortable hotel – . . . . than I'd expected for the price.
6. She was quite young – . . . . than I was expecting.

Now look at this example:

The curry was quite hot – but not as hot as I was expecting.

Complete these sentences as in the example.

7. It was quite difficult – . . . .
8. The theatre was quite full – . . . .
9. The sea was quite warm – . . . .
10. There were quite a few people there – . . . .

12 Must've (CB page 109)

We often use *must've* + past participle to guess about past events. Complete the short dialogues below with the correct form of the verbs in the box.

be	go	leave
get	join	switch

1. A: Is Steve still here? I can't find him anywhere.
   B: I think he must've . . . . home early.
2. A: And then, after that, we went for a meal in the Grand Hotel.
   B: That must've . . . . expensive.
3. A: I can't find my purse. I hope I haven't lost it.
   B: You must've . . . . it at home. Don't worry.
4. A: I phoned you earlier, but there was no answer.
   B: Oh, I must've . . . . my mobile off by accident. Sorry.
5. A: Is that Chris getting out of that BMW?
   B: Yes, he must've . . . . a new car. Let's go and have a look.
6. A: Tim's looking very fit, isn't he? He's lost weight.
   B: Yes, he must've . . . . a gym or started jogging or something.

16 Films and television

1 At the cinema (CB page 110)

Complete the sentences below with the words in the box.

credits	interval	rows	subtitles
dubbed	matinee	screen	trailers

I always go to the cinema in the evening. I don't like
(1) .... performances; there's no atmosphere. I
get there early so I can sit where I want – about ten
(2) .... from the front, right in the middle.
That way you get the best view of the (3) ....
I sit down with my popcorn and get ready for the
(4) ...., you know, when they show you films
which are coming out later in the year. I love those. I
don't mind films with (5) ...., but I can't stand
films which are (6) .... – the people just look
silly. Most films these days aren't long enough to need
a(n) (7) ...., but if there is one, I get fresh
supplies of popcorn and an ice cream. Most people
leave as soon as the film finishes, but I like to stay and
read the (8) .... to see who all the actors
were. I suppose I'm a bit of a nerd when it comes to
films, really!

2 Water metaphors (CB page 112)

In the Robocop text in the Coursebook, you
read that Mary Whitehouse wanted to 'protect
children from the filth and violence that is
flooding our TV screens'. We often use words
connected with water in a metaphorical way.

Look at the verbs in the box and check their
meanings in a dictionary.

dry up	overflow	surge
flood	pour	trickle

Now choose the correct alternative.

1. It was a great party. There were so many people, we
   were *trickling / overflowing* into the garden.
2. Our business has had a website for a couple of years
   and in the first six months orders were just slowly
   pouring / trickling in, but recently we've been *flooded /
   poured* with new orders and enquiries. I guess more
   people are starting to hear about us.

3. We used to get a lot of orders through our website,
   but recently they've really *surged / dried up*. I don't
   know what we're doing wrong.
4. When famine or war affects a country, you always
   get thousands of refugees *pouring / trickling* into
   neighbouring countries in desperate need of food
   and shelter.
5. I was just standing there, waiting for the train. There
   were loads of people, and when the train arrived,
   suddenly, everybody just *overflowed / surged* forward
   and I nearly got squashed against the side of the
   train.

**Now write the correct verb from the box next to
these ideas.**

a. a small stream in the middle of summer with hardly
   any water in it   ....
b. a stream with no water in it at all   ....
c. a river bursts its banks and people have to leave
   their homes   ....
d. a pot of tea   ....
e. too much tea in the cup   ....
f. a mountain stream that comes suddenly with a huge
   amount of water   ....

3 -ed adjectives (CB page 112)

In the Robocop text, people were shocked by the
TV version of the film. Complete the sentences
below with the words in the box.

annoyed	disappointed	pleased
delighted	excited	shocked

1. The film wasn't as good as I was expecting. I was a
   bit ...., to be honest.
2. That film should be for adults only. I was quite
   .... by some of the violence.
3. Our eldest son, Keith, and his girlfriend have decided
   to get married. We're absolutely ....
4. We're off to New York on Saturday. I'm really
   .... I've never been there before.
5. Do you want to see what I've painted? I'm really
   .... with it.
6. The newspaper said the film started at seven, but
   actually it started at 6.45, so I missed the first ten
   minutes. How can they make a mistake like that? I
   was really ....

Now match the *-ed* adjectives 7–12 to the situations a–f.

7. frustrated ☐
8. relieved ☐
9. puzzled ☐
10. confused ☐
11. worried ☐
12. amazed ☐

a. You've just passed your driving test.

b. You've been stuck in a traffic jam for an hour.

c. Your twelve-year-old daughter should have been home an hour ago.

d. A friend leaves without saying goodbye.

e. You can't understand the difference between a PC and a Mac.

f. You've just heard that your boss has been arrested for shoplifting.

Hidden collocations

When you do an exercise like the one above, try to notice the language used. Complete these expressions.

13. not as good as I was ....

14. .... a mistake

15. .... your driving test

16. the difference .... X and Y

17. arrested .... shoplifting

18. .... in a traffic jam

4 The best film I've ever …

Complete the sentences below with the words in the box.

done	experienced	had (x2)	heard
made (x2)	met	seen	visited

1. It's the best film I've ever ....

2. It's the best place I've ever ....

3. It's the best decision I've ever ....

4. It was the worst weather I'd ever ....

5. It was the worst experience I'd ever ....

6. It's the hardest thing I've ever ....

7. It's the biggest mistake I've ever ....

8. That's the most ridiculous thing I've ever ....

9. It was the best meal I've ever ....

10. She was one of the most interesting people I've ever ....

5 Past perfect (CB page 113)

Put the verbs in brackets in the past simple or the past perfect. Then compare your version with the one in the answer key. Sometimes there is a choice of tense.

A managing director went to see his doctor because he was so stressed he couldn't sleep. All the workers at his factory (1) .... (go) on strike because they (2) .... (want) better pay and conditions. The director (3) .... (already / try) sleeping pills but they (4) .... (work). The doctor (5) .... (advise) him to lie very still in bed and count sheep. The next day, the director (6) .... (return) to see the doctor, who (7) .... (ask): 'How did you get on? Any success?'

'I'm afraid not,' said the director. 'By the time I (8) .... (count) the twenty-fifth sheep, they (9) .... (all / go) on strike for shorter hours and lower fences.'

6 Prepositional phrases

Complete the sentences below with the words and phrases in the box.

behind	in front of	next to	on the floor
on top of	out of the way	over	to the left

I was sitting there, eating my popcorn, just as the film was starting, when this tall man came and sat right (1) .... me, so I couldn't see the screen. There was no-one sitting (2) .... me, so I moved one place (3) .... , but then a little girl (4) .... me said, 'I can't see,' so I had to move again and I dropped my popcorn (5) .... Somebody shouted, 'Get (6) ....,' as I looked for somewhere else to sit and the only place left was in the row in front, next to the big man. So I climbed (7) .... the seat and sat down – right (8) .... his hot dog and coke.

Joke

A: I'm sure I recognise you. Haven't I seen your face somewhere else?
B: I don't think so. It's always been here on the front of my head.

7 Typical mistakes

Here are some typical mistakes with prepositions. Can you correct them?

1. I'm going to home. See you tomorrow.

   ....

2. I'm going in Ireland next summer.

   ....

3. I live nearby the coast.

   ....

4. The bank's opposite of the post office.

   ....

5. Go along the street and turn to left.

   ....

6. Did you come with the bus?

   ....

7. No, I came with foot.

   ....

8. That's typical for you!

   ....

8 Expressions with *out of*

Complete the sentences below with the expressions in the box.

out of control	out of fashion
out of my depth	out of petrol
out of sight	out of the question
out of work	out of your mind

1. Keep your eyes open for a garage. We're nearly
   ....

2. The good news is that the number of people
   .... is actually decreasing.

3. I went to a wine-tasting evening the other day. Everybody except me seemed to know a lot about wine. I felt totally ....

4. If you're going out in this storm, you must be
   ....

5. I'm sorry, but there's no way I can visit the Madrid office and the Bilbao office on the same day. It's
   ....

6. This year black is in fashion; next year it'll be
   ....

7. We watched for over an hour till the ship went
   .... over the horizon.

8. We hit a patch of ice and the car spun round and round ....

Have you ever tried to buy a book only to find it is *out of print*? It's frustrating, isn't it?

Do you get *out of breath* easily? Maybe you should join a gym!

9 Mixed conditionals (CB page 119)

Complete these sentences with the correct form of the words in brackets.

1. If we hadn't moved last year, we .... in that awful, smelly flat. (still / live)

2. If I hadn't had such a good time going to parties when I was at university, I .... a good degree and a decent job now. (probably / have)

3. My parents moved from France to England when I was only four. If they'd stayed there until I was a bit older, I .... really good French. (probably / able to speak)

4. If I hadn't spent so much time chatting, I .... the bus, and I .... here now trying to get a taxi. (not miss, not stand)

5. I wouldn't be a manager today if it .... for the support and encouragement I received when I first joined the company. (not be)

6. It would have been almost impossible to buy a house if my parents .... me some money. (not lend)

7. I would never have known what love is if you .... into my life, darling! (not come)

8. You'd have a better social life if you .... the last ten years building up your business and forgetting to live. (not spend)

7 Cars and cities

1 *If* suggestions (CB page 122)

Make sentence starters by putting the words in the right order. Begin as shown.

1. really / be / would / great / it / if / they
   It ....
2. more / it'd / be / they / if / useful
   It'd ....
3. if / they / better / far / be / it'd
   It'd ....
4. what / good / be / would / really / they / is / if
   What ....

Match the *if* sentences 5–8 to the contexts a–d.

5. It'd be far better if they banned it completely. ☐
6. It'd be really great if they opened it up to the public more often. ☐
7. It'd be more useful if they developed a tram system or something like that. ☐
8. What would be really good is if they let us wear jeans and casual clothes occasionally. ☐

a. traffic problems
b. Buckingham Palace
c. smoking on trains
d. work

2 Auxiliary verbs

Emphatic *do/does*
In the conversation in the Coursebook on page 121, you heard:

It does seem a funny place for a crossing.
That does make it difficult to see.

Make these examples more emphatic by adding *do* or *does* once in each sentence.

1. I don't like swimming, but I like going to the beach just to sunbathe.
2. It's not the best film I've ever seen, but it gets more interesting towards the end.
3. I know you're annoyed, but I think you're over-reacting a bit.
4. It seems pretty cheap, but then again it has a little scratch on it.
5. I don't mind people being late when they can't help it, but I mind when people are late and they think it doesn't matter.
6. Cambridge is a great place to live, but it gets a bit crowded in the summer.
7. The speed that cars go round here worries me. They should do something about it.

3 Cars

Label the pictures of the cars with the words in the box below.

Inside the car: accelerator, brake, clutch, dashboard, gear stick, glove, compartment, handbrake
Outside the car: aerial, bonnet, boot, tyre, wheel, windscreen, wing mirror

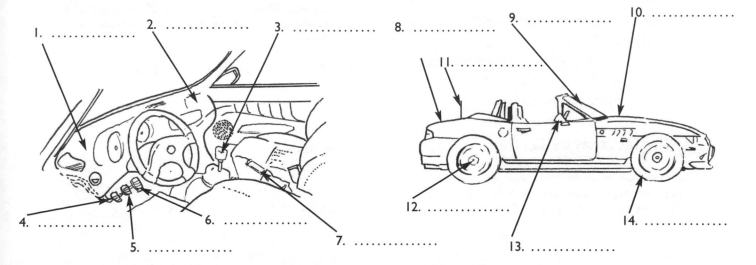

1. ....
2. ....
3. ....
4. ....
5. ....
6. ....
7. ....
8. ....
9. ....
10. ....
11. ....
12. ....
13. ....
14. ....

4 Traffic signs

Complete these sentences with a suitable word.

1. Watch . . . . for elderly people.

2. You're in a 40 mile-an-hour . . . .

3. You're approaching an accident . . . . spot.

4. The . . . . carriageway is about to end.

5. Beware . . . . deer or other . . . . animals on the road.

6. You are approaching a . . . . crossing.

Check your answers in the answer key.

5 Traffic offences

Complete the sentences below with the words in the box.

drink	fine	light
seatbelt	speeding	ticket

1. I got caught . . . . last week. I was doing forty-five in a built-up area.
2. I got a parking . . . . this morning. I admit I shouldn't have been there, but I was only there for five minutes.
3. A friend of mine went through a red . . . . and got a fifty-pound . . . .
4. Did you know that if you're caught not wearing a . . . . , you get fined automatically?
5. . . . . -driving is a serious crime.

6 The fact that (CB page 121)

In the conversation in the Coursebook, you heard: 'The other problem with it is the fact that lots of cars park all round there.'

We use *the fact that* a lot in spoken English to emphasise our point. Re-write these sentences with *the fact that* in a suitable place.

1. What really annoys me is the government knows there's a problem, but doesn't want to do anything about it.

. . . .
. . . .

2. The thing that really annoys me is nobody takes us seriously.

. . . .
. . . .

3. A: People should leave their cars at home and use the bus more often.
   B: You're forgetting some people don't live near a regular bus service, though.

. . . .
. . . .

4. The reason I don't take the bus more often is they never arrive on time.

. . . .
. . . .

The fact that **can also start a sentence:**

The fact that I can't speak German doesn't mean I can't get a job in Germany.

Make a sentence about yourself like this:

The fact that I can't … doesn't mean I …

7 Compound adjectives

Notice these examples:

He earned fifty pounds.
He got a fifty-pound fine.

We say *fifty pounds* but *a fifty-pound fine*. The noun (pound) is singular when used in a compound adjective like this. Make compound adjectives by matching the words 1–8 to the words a–h.

1.	a ten-year	a.	holiday
2.	a two-week	b.	engine
3.	a two-litre	c.	fine
4.	a seven-day-a-week	d.	boy
5.	an eight-hour	e.	limit
6.	a three-year-old	f.	job
7.	a thirty-mile-an-hour	g.	jail sentence
8.	a £200	h.	day

Complete these sentences with the compound adjectives you formed.

9. We're just back from .... in Thailand.

10. I work ...., Monday to Friday.

11. We've got .... and another child on the way.

12. He got .... for the murder and two years for the burglary.

13. Don't you think you should slow down a bit? After all, there's .... in town!

14. It's an average-sized car, with ...., but it's pretty economical.

15. I only got .... and a warning to be more careful in future.

16. Looking after children is ...., twenty-four-hour-a-day .... !

8 Make, let

Notice the verb pattern: *make/let* + object + verb.

My parents made me apologise.
My teacher let me leave early.

Complete this text with the correct form of *make* or *let*.

When I was about fifteen, my parents (1) ....
my uncle take me to watch a professional football
match about fifty miles away by coach. It was an
evening game and on the way back, the coach stopped
at a service station to (2) .... people use the
toilet. Unfortunately, some of the men damaged some
cars in the car park and somebody stole some things
from the shop. Ten minutes later, going along the
motorway, two police cars overtook the coach and
(3) .... it stop. The police (4) .... everybody
get off the coach so that they could look for the
stolen things. Then they took everyone to the police
station for questioning. When we got there, they
(5) .... us take our shoes off before putting us
in the cells. After about half an hour, they interviewed
me and fortunately, they (6) .... me phone my
parents to tell them what had happened. They finally
(7) .... some of us go about six o'clock the
following morning. The whole experience was quite
frightening. My parents never (8) .... me travel
to a football match like that again.

9 The passive (CB page 124)

Present perfect
Complete the sentences below with the correct passive form of the verbs in the box.

not invite	postpone	re-decorate
definitely / send	steal	you / vaccinate

1. A: Is the meeting at two o'clock?
   B: Actually, it .... It's going to be tomorrow instead.

2. A: Are you going to Christoph's wedding?
   B: I'd like to, but I ....

3. My bicycle .... I left it outside, but it's gone.

4. Our office .... and it looks really smart.

5. You say you haven't received my fax. I can assure you it ....

6. .... against TB?

Will
Complete the sentences below with the correct passive form of the verbs in the box.

decide	drive	fly	give	pick up

M is giving James Bond instructions for his next mission.

7. You .... at the airport and .... to your hotel by Natasha – our beautiful Polish agent.

8. At the hotel, you .... a suitcase with further instructions and $1 billion.

9. That evening, you .... by helicopter to the mountains to meet Dr Schultz.

10. He will exchange the microchip for the money. The future of the world .... by the success of this mission, 007.

Be, must, can, should
Complete the sentences below with the correct form of the verbs in the box. The sentences are taken from hotel and restaurant situations.

clean	include	order	serve
hand in	lock	purchase	vacate

11. Service is not . . . .

12. Breakfast is . . . . between 7 am and 10 am.

13. Rooms are . . . . between 10 am and 1 pm.

14. Rooms must be . . . . by 11 am on the day of departure and keys . . . . to Reception.

15. Light meals and snacks can be . . . . from Room Service by dialling 02.

16. Drinks can be . . . . from your mini-bar.

17. Valuables should be . . . . in the safety deposit box in your room.

How many passives are there in the joke below? Underline them.

> **Joke**
>
> A man went to a hospital for a new brain. He was given a choice between two brains – a pilot's for £30,000 or a politician's for £100,000.
>
> 'Does that mean the politician's brain is better?' asked the man.
>
> 'Not exactly,' replied the doctor. 'It's because the politician's brain has never been used.'

10   Expressions with *all* (CB page 121)

In the conversation in the Coursebook, Claire said: '… lots of cars park all round there.' *All* can be used to give emphasis in expressions. For example:

I was alone.
I was all alone. (totally alone)

It's your fault.
It's all your fault. (You are completely responsible for it.)

Re-write these sentence with *all* in the correct place.

1. We had to start over again.

   . . . .

2. It's sad. He lives by himself and no one visits him as far as I know.

   . . . .

3. And they kept playing loud dance music through the night.

   . . . .

4. There were hundreds of bicycles along the side of the road.

   . . . .

5. A: Have you phoned Patrick yet?
   B: Oh no! I forgot about it.

   . . . .

6. His new novel is about wartime Italy.

   . . . .

7. I'm sorry. It's my fault.

   . . . .

8. When you saw the ghost, were you alone?

   . . . .

All is also part of fixed expressions. Complete the short dialogues below with the expressions in the box.

all being well	all of a sudden
all in all	all over the place

9. A: So, what happened next?
   B: Well, ... , there was this sort of flash and smoke started pouring out of the engine – the car was on fire.

10. A: Welcome back. Did you have a good holiday?
    B: The weather was a bit disappointing, but . . . . , we had a good time, thanks.

11. A: Is your son's bedroom a mess as well?
    B: Terrible. There's clothes, magazines, coffee cups and CDs . . . . A typical teenager!

12. A: What time are you planning to arrive?
    B: . . . . , about six o'clock. It depends what time I can get away from work.

> **Language note**
>
> The expressions with *all* above show you how important it is to learn expressions as whole chunks. There is no 'rule' about *all*. You just have to learn lots of expressions containing *all*.

11 Agreeing expressions (CB page 123)

Make expressions for agreeing by putting the words in the correct order. Begin as shown.

1. that's / think / what / I / exactly

   That's ....

2. more / agree / couldn't / I

   I ....

3. yes, / what / I / mean / you / know

   Yes, ...

4. about / me / tell / it / !

   Tell ....

5. say / can / again / you / that

   You ....

6. the / words / you / my / mouth / took / right / out / of

   You ....

12 Writing: a balanced composition

Car owners who wish to drive into some city centres now have to pay a £5 fee to enter those areas during working hours. Discuss the main advantages and disadvantages of this.

Sample composition
Complete the composition below with the words and phrases in the box.

clear-cut issue	for example	knock-on effect
encouraging	increasing all the time	results in

With the number of cars in cities (1) ...., action to reduce congestion and the pollution that comes with it is vital. However, charging car owners to enter city centres at certain times has both advantages and disadvantages.

The first obvious advantage is it encourages people to leave their cars at home. Fewer cars on the road (2) .... better traffic flow and everybody gets to their destination much quicker. (3) A(n) .... is that noise and pollution should be significantly reduced. Another advantage is that the money collected from those who still drive can be used to improve public transport and even reduce prices, (4) .... even more people to use those services.

The main disadvantage is that many people rely on their cars to get to work and cannot switch to public transport easily. (5) ...., parents may need to use the car to drop off their children at school before going on to work. There isn't time for them to then park and catch a bus. Others have jobs that would be almost impossible without a car to get them from A to B during the day. Why should these people have to pay extra just for carrying out their daily tasks?

This is not a(n) (6)............... . Although the benefits of this kind of scheme are very real, there are a number of cases that should be given special consideration, and perhaps a smaller charge, or no charge could be applied in some circumstances.

Write a composition on the following:
'Some companies are encouraging employees who drive to work to "car share". So people who drive to work on a similar route are now encouraged to travel together, using one car one week, the other car the next week and so on. Discuss the main advantages and disadvantages of this system.'

18 Annoying things

1 Verb collocations (CB page 126)

Look back at paragraph four of the 'sticky problem' text in the Coursebook. Then complete the extract below with the correct form of the verbs in the box.

ban	bring	get	stick
break	delay	reinforce	tackle

Darlington isn't the first place in the world to try to (1) . . . . the sticky issue of chewing gum. In 1992, the Asian city of Singapore (2) . . . . all eating and importing of chewing gum after it was claimed trains had been (3) . . . . because trapped chewing gum caused the automatic doors to (4) . . . . The ban came with severe penalties for (5) . . . . the law. Smugglers (6) . . . . gum into the country could (7) . . . . a jail sentence of one year plus an eight-thousand-dollar fine. The government also tried to (8) . . . . its message with advertising campaigns, which included slogans such as, 'If you can't think because you can't chew, try a banana'.

Now check your answers in the Coursebook.

2 Collocations: *issue*

Verb + *issue*
Complete the sentences below with the correct form of the verbs in the box.

avoid	clarify	complicate	tackle

1. It's not really a problem at all. I think you are . . . . the issue.
2. You've got to meet this problem head-on and make a decision. You can't keep . . . . the issue.
3. There are one or two things I need you to explain to . . . . the issue. It's all a bit confusing at the moment.
4. The government has no clear plan on how it is going to . . . . the growing issue of homelessness.

Adjective + *issue*
Complete the sentences below with the adjectives in the box.

controversial	environmental	political	real

5. Greenpeace is concerned with raising awareness of . . . . issues, such as the reduction of rainforests and excessive whale hunting.
6. Human cloning is, and will remain for many years, a highly . . . . issue.
7. In all the controversy about the amount of traffic in city centres, parking problems and congestion, the . . . . issue is being forgotten – how to improve public transport to such an extent that people will not even consider taking their cars to work.
8. Terrorism, and the threat of terrorism, is the most important . . . . issue facing governments today.

3 Phrasal verbs (CB page 127)

Complete these sentences with *down, up* or *out*. Notice that in some of the phrasal verbs, the particle does not change the basic meaning of the verb, but adds emphasis. For example:

He saved £1000.
He saved up £1000. (almost identical in meaning)

I'm tired.
I'm tired out. (very tired, exhausted)

1. Come on, hurry . . . . or we're going to be late.
2. I can't sit out in this sun any longer. I'm going inside to cool . . . .
3. Come on, we'd better drink . . . . The pub closes in five minutes.
4. Work is mad at the moment. I'm getting quite stressed . . . .
5. The city tour is brilliant. After seeing all the sights, you end . . . . in a lovely café next to the river and they give you a free drink.
6. I'm trying not to spend much money at the moment because I'm saving . . . . for a new car. The clutch on my old one has completely worn . . . .
7. Getting annoyed isn't going to help, so please try and calm . . . . and then we can talk about it properly.

8. I'm tired . . . . after all that walking. Let's have a nice cup of tea.

9. A: Can I borrow your mobile for a minute?

   B: It's not working. I've used . . . . all my call time. I need to get another voucher.

10. A: So, it's Mr Jonson – j–o–n–s–o–n.

    B: No, Johnson. You've missed . . . . the 'h'.

11. Slow . . . . a bit. I think we turn left somewhere around here.

12. Can you check these figures for me? I think I've added them . . . . OK, but I just want someone to look at them.

13. A: Where do you want to eat tonight?

    B: Well, actually, I'd quite like to try . . . . that new Australian restaurant. It sounds really unusual.

14. The reason I don't want a party at my place is that I'll be the one who has to clean . . . . all the mess next morning.

4 Complaining (CB page 128)

When we complain about things or wish things were different, we sometimes use *wish* + *would*. For example:

I wish they'd get the lift fixed.
I wish they'd do something about all the rubbish on the streets.

Complain about these work situations with *wish* + *would* and the words in brackets.

1. The office is too hot in summer.
   (install air-conditioning)
   I wish they . . . .

2. There aren't enough parking spaces. (provide more)
   I wish they . . . .

3. The computer system keeps crashing. (update)
   I wish they . . . .

4. It would be nice to have a Christmas party.
   (organise)
   I wish someone . . . .

5. It would be better if the place looked brighter.
   (re-decorate)
   I wish they . . . .

6. There's hardly any training. (increase the amount)
   I wish they . . . .

7. Our salaries haven't changed for two years. (give us a pay rise)
   I wish they . . . .

8. Our MD is incompetent. (get rid of him)
   I wish they . . . .

Glad, pleased, delighted
When things change for the better, we often say:

I'm glad they've fixed it at last.
I'm pleased they've decided to meet again.

Re-write the sentences 1–8 beginning *I'm glad/I'm pleased/I'm delighted*. Use the present perfect.

9. I'm glad . . . .

10. I'm pleased . . . .

11. I'm glad . . . .

12. I'm delighted . . . .

13. I'm glad . . . .

14. I'm pleased . . . .

15. I'm glad . . . .

16. I'm delighted . . . .

5 Complaining and apologising

The sentences below were said by a complaining hotel guest and the hotel receptionist. Who said what? Write G for guest or R for receptionist.

1. I'll see if I can do something about it.   . . . . .

2. I'd be grateful if you could do something about it.   . . . . .

3. This is the second time I've asked you.   . . . . .

4. I'll mention this to the manager.   . . . . .

5. I want to speak to the manager.   . . . . .

6. I'm terribly sorry, sir/madam.   . . . . .

7. Please accept our apologies.   . . . . .

8. I'll sort it out straightaway.   . . . . .

9. I'm not very happy about it.   . . . . .

10. This isn't good enough.   . . . . .

6 Explain, ask

Which sentence with *explain* is wrong?

1a. She explained everything.

1b. She explained it very clearly/badly.

1c. She explained that it was a computer error.

1d. She explained me that she had made a mistake.

1e. She explained the situation.

1f. She explained why she had done it.

Which sentence with *ask* is wrong?

2a. He asked me to explain.

2b. He asked me about my relationship with you.

2c. He asked me if I was still at college.

2d. He asked me why I was visiting the US.

2e. He asked me for a lift.

2f. He asked me that I would help him.

7 Was/were going to (CB page 128)

We often use *was/were going out* to talk about changing our plans. Match the beginnings 1–6 to the endings a–f.

1. I was going to come by train, but
2. I was going to buy a new pair of shoes, but
3. I was going to travel round the world, but
4. I was going to buy you a present, but
5. I was going to buy you a Rolex, but
6. I was going to ring you, but

a. they didn't have my size.
b. it was much cheaper by coach.
c. I just couldn't find anything you'd like.
d. then I met Jeff and we got married.
e. I just couldn't find a phone.
f. then I saw the price!

Look at this common pattern:

I thought you said you were going to …

Re-write the sentences 1–6 above using this pattern. The first one has been done for you.

7. *I thought you said you were going to come by train.*
8. ....
9. ....
10. ....
11. ....
12. ....

Which sentence contains a mistake? Correct it by crossing out one word.

13a. I thought you said me you were going to come at seven.

13b. I thought you told me you were going to come at seven.

8 Jokes: complaining

Complete the three jokes below with the lines in the box.

- I just moved the potato and there it was.
- I'm sorry, sir. I'll take it away and bring you something that is.
- Then why aren't you laughing?

1. Customer: Waiter! This food isn't fit for a pig!
   Waiter: ....
2. Customer: Waiter, this soup tastes funny.
   Waiter: ....
3. Waiter: How did you find the steak, sir?
   Customer: ....

9 Collocations: *problem*

Verb + *problem*
Complete the sentences below with the correct form of the verbs in the box.

deal with	foresee	run into	underestimate

1. Is this a problem you can .... on your own or do you need my help?
2. This is more serious than I first thought. I obviously .... the problem.
3. The deadline for this project is 30 June. Do you .... any problems with that?
4. I'm afraid I won't have the new website ready for you on Friday. I'm really sorry, but I .... a few problems with the database.

Adjective + *problem*
Complete the sentences below with the adjectives in the box.

actual	common	major	minor

5. Can you explain all that again because I'm still not sure what the .... problem is?
6. I've had a look at your car and it's nothing to worry about. It's only a(n) .... problem with the electrics. I'll fix it in no time. In fact, it's quite a(n) .... problem with this type of car.
7. We had to move house because we had .... problems with the neighbours. They were an absolute nightmare!

10 Writing 1: a letter of complaint

Sample letter
Complete the letter below with the words and expressions in the box.

despite	finally		firstly	immediately
in order to	needless to say	nor		secondly

Dear Sir/Madam,

I am writing to complain about a number of problems we had on a holiday that was booked through your company. The holiday was from 4th–11th this year, at the Miramar Apartments in Santa Ponsa. Our booking reference was MRL SP 379. I list the complaints below.

(1)............, your brochure claims that all the apartments in the Miramar have balconies, but ours did not, and no other rooms were free so we were unable to move to an apartment that had one.

(2)............, the air-conditioning broke down on our second day and nobody came to fix it until our last day, (3)............ repeated requests to the apartment manager and your representative. (4)............, the temperature at night was unbearable.

(5)............, our transfer to the airport was supposed to be by taxi, already paid for as part of the package price, but it never arrived and we had to call another one (6)........... get to the airport in time. Neither the apartment manager (7)............ your representative were available to help us with this serious problem. The taxi cost 25 Euros, which we expect to have refunded to us (8)........... . I enclose the receipt.

I look forward to receiving the refund for the taxi fare and your reaction to these issues, and how you plan to address them.

Yours faithfully,

Robert McBride

Write a letter of complaint about a holiday you took, based on the sample letter above. Use these notes.

The brochure mentions a tennis court, but there wasn't one – you had taken all your tennis things.

The beach was a forty-five-minute walk, not a ten-minute walk – a ninety-minute round trip and you were exhausted by the end of each day.

The lock on your apartment door was broken and it wasn't fixed until the last day – you spent all day worrying that something would be stolen.

11 Writing 2: a complaint anecdote

Describe a situation when you had to complain – perhaps in a restaurant, hotel or shop. Here are some ideas to help you.

In a hotel
Once, I was staying in a hotel in (Rio) and …
I'd asked for a room with a balcony.
The room hadn't been cleaned.
The bathroom was filthy.
I couldn't sleep because of the noise.
So I decided to speak to the … who said/explained that …
But I still wasn't happy because … , so I …

In a shop
I'd decided to buy a …
When I got it home, I realised it was broken/the wrong colour/the wrong size.
When I plugged it in, it wouldn't work.
I took it back and spoke to …
They replaced it immediately/They refused to replace it.
I decided to write to the …

In a restaurant
Once, I was having lunch/dinner in a restaurant in … and …
I discovered a … in my …
The food was cold/undercooked/burnt.
I ordered a … , but they brought me a …
I called the waiter who …
I insisted on speaking to the manager.
In the end, I decided to …

19 Your future

1 Starting with *what* (CB page 134)

Make sentences by matching the beginnings 1–8 to the endings a–h.

1. What'd I'd really like to do is to write
2. What I want to do most is to travel
3. What I'm hoping to do is get
4. What I'm planning to do this year is learn
5. What I need to do is start
6. What I hope will happen is I'll meet
7. What I'm thinking about doing is
8. What I'd really like is to spend

a. a job on a ship for a year.
b. six months learning to fly.
c. how to drive.
d. saving a bit of money.
e. round the world for a year.
f. spending a year in a different country.
g. the man/woman of my dreams.
h. a book about my childhood.

2 I might try and ... (CB page 134)

In the Coursebook, in Using vocabulary, Exercise 1, you read: 'I might try and get a job as a chef.' This is a common pattern in spoken English. Another is: 'I might go and ... .' Match the situations 1–8 to the thoughts a–h.

1. Eric's thinking about becoming a chef.
2. Simon's got a Spanish girlfriend.
3. A friend of yours is in hospital.
4. Kath is thinking of giving up cigarettes.
5. Rob is going to have his left ear pierced.
6. Lisa needs to lose about ten kilos.
7. Eve wants a car, but hasn't got enough money.
8. John is fed up doing the same job for the last ten years. He's thirty-three.

a. I might try and get a job in Spain.
b. I might go and do a catering course.
c. I might go and join a gym.
d. I might go and get mine done, too.
e. I might try and give up.
f. I might go and see her.
g. I might try and get a bank loan.
h. I might try and re-train and do something completely different.

Now match these follow-up thoughts i–viii to the comments a–h above.

i. If I don't, she'll probably find a local boy.
ii. If I do, my parents will be mad with me.
iii. If I don't, I'd better go on a crash diet.
iv. If I don't, I'll go mad.
v. If I don't, I know I'll damage my health.
vi. If I don't get one, I'll have to get an evening job.
vii. If I don't, I think I'll go and work in a restaurant anyway.
viii. If I do, I must remember to get her some grapes or flowers or something.

3 Planning structures

I'd quite like to ...
Notice this pattern of two linked clauses:

I'd quite like to come with you, but I'm not sure if I'll have enough time.

Complete the sentences below with *I'd quite like to* and the ideas in the box.

apply for the manager's job	be able to play the piano
have a month in the sun	train as a nurse
work in the UK	

1. ...., but I'm not sure if I'll be able to get the time off.

2. ...., but I'm not sure if I'll get it.

3. ...., but I'm not sure if my English is good enough.

4. ...., but I'm not sure if I want to work long hours.

5. ...., but I'm not sure if I've got the patience to learn.

I'm quite interested in ...
Which ending is wrong? Cross it out.

I'm quite interested in doing a law course, but ...

a. I'm not sure if it's a good idea.

b. I'm not sure to do it or not.

c. I'm not sure about it.

d. I'm not sure whether to do it or not.

e. I'm not sure I should do it.

Now make sentences by matching the beginnings 6–10 to the endings f–j.

6. I'm quite interested in taking up squash, ☐

7. I'm quite interested in music, ☐

8. I'm quite interested in going to China, ☐

9. I'm quite interested in studying medicine, ☐

10. I'm quite interested in Liz, ☐

f. but I don't think I can afford to at the moment.

g. but I don't know if she's interested in me.

h. but I'm not into classical stuff.

i. but I'm not sure if I'm really fit enough.

j. but I'm not sure whether I'll get the qualifications I need or not.

4 **Sentence adverbs** (CB page 137)

What are these sentence adverbs? Complete the words.

a. ev_ _ t _ _ lly

b. ho _ _ f _ _ ly

c. b _ _ _ cally

d. id _ _ _ ly

e. rea _ _ st _ _ ally

Complete these sentences with the most suitable sentence adverb.

1. ...., I'd like to retire when I'm fifty, but ...., I'll probably have to work until I'm sixty.

2. I've got my final exams in the summer, which .... I'll pass.

3. ...., everyone just wants to be happy, don't they?

4. I do a bit of photography in my spare time, but I'd like to do it professionally ....

Notice that *ideally* and *realistically* often come together when we talk about what we would like to happen. A similar pair is *in theory*/*theoretically*, and *in practice*. For example:

In theory, there's no reason why your idea shouldn't work, but in practice I don't think it will.

5 **If expressions** (CB page 137)

Can you remember these *if* expressions? First make the expressions by putting the words in the correct order and complete the sentences. Someone is talking about where they live.

1. ...., I'll be moving into my new flat next week. (if / goes / all / well)

2. ...., a friend of mine from work is going to rent my spare room, which will help pay the bills. (if / goes / according / to / everything / plan)

3. ...., I know someone else who might be interested. (if / falls / that / through)

4. ...., I'll just have to put an advert in the local newspaper. (if / else / all / fails)

6 If things …

We often talk about the future starting like this:

If things work out between us, then …

What does *things* refers to? Match the sentences 1–5 to the ideas a–e.

1. If things get any worse, make an appointment to see me again. □
2. If things don't improve, I'm going to start looking for another job. □
3. If things don't work out, I'll have to go back and live with my parents. □
4. If things change, I'll give you a ring and we'll arrange another time – otherwise, I'll see you next Wednesday. □
5. If things stay like this for much longer, I'll just have to tell him it's over. □

a. my living arrangements
b. my plans
c. my job situation
d. my relationship with my boyfriend
e. your health

7 Just do it! (CB page 133)

In the conversation in the Coursebook, you heard: 'Why don't we just go off somewhere?' *Just* is very often part of a common expression. Mark where you would usually find *just* in these sentences.

1. I don't understand how it happened.
2. Yes, I'm ready. I'll get my coat.
3. If you could sign at the bottom, please.
4. Can I ask you something?
5. I want to thank you for all your help.
6. A: How much does this one cost?
   B: Hold on, I'll check.
7. Don't sit there! Do something!
8. Don't worry. It's a wasp.
9. That's what I think myself.
10. It's the wind.
11. Why don't you resign?
12. I'll check in the timetable.
13. Will your computer switch itself off?
14. Is it too warm in here or is it me?
15. What did you say?

8 Present perfect for the future

Complete the sentences below with the correct form of the verbs in the box. The first one is done for you.

check	get off	pay off	try
~~finish~~	pass	save up	work out

1. A: Can I have a look at your newspaper?
   B: Yes, you can have it as soon as I've *finished* with it.
2. A: Are you having fun with your new computer?
   B: Well, I will be, once I .... how the printer works. I just can't get it to work.
3. You'll love salsa dancing once you .... it. It's brilliant.
4. I'll let you know the dates as soon as I .... with the travel agent.
5. Make sure you keep your ticket until after you .... the train.
6. Once I .... my driving test, I'm going to buy myself a sports car.
7. I'll be a lot happier when I .... my car loan. It's £259 a month.
8. The minute I .... enough money, I'm going travelling in the Far East.

9 Future collocations

Make sentences by matching the beginnings 1–6 to the endings a–f.

1. I can see myself going □
2. I can see myself getting □
3. I can see myself spending □
4. I can't see myself getting □
5. I can't see myself staying □
6. I can't see myself doing □

a. a year doing voluntary work.
b. abroad eventually.
c. married for a few years yet.
d. at home for much longer.
e. the same job for more than five years.
f. a job in the media.

Language note

The pattern in Exercise 9 is used to talk about the future without using a future tense. There are lots of ways of talking about the future:
I'm about to …
I'm certain to …
It's possible that …
We might …

10 Collocations

Plans
Match the sentences 1–4 to their meanings a–d.

1. My plans have fallen through.
2. My plans are beginning to taking shape.
3. My plans are really coming together.
4. My plans are up in the air at the moment.

a. Things are going really well.
b. Things are starting to look good.
c. Something went wrong.
d. Things are very uncertain.

Opportunity
Complete the sentences below with the words in the box.

every	find	lifetime	many	much

5. Go to Australia! It's the opportunity of a(n) .... !
6. We must .... an opportunity to visit my sister.
7. Living out in the country, we don't get .... opportunity to go to the theatre.
8. You should try to speak English at .... opportunity.
9. There aren't as .... opportunities for school leavers today as there were when I left school.

Which collocation with *opportunity* is wrong?

10a. a great opportunity
10b. a rare opportunity
10c. a small opportunity
10d. a golden opportunity
10e. a missed opportunity

Future
Complete the sentences below with the words in the box.

career	events	president
date	generations	reference

11. Check out our website for details of all current and future ....
12. You don't need to read it now, but put it somewhere safe for future ....
13. There may not be enough natural resources for future .... unless we do something now.
14. I have no idea what my future .... will be. I'll probably end up in computers or something like that.

15. He's a talented and ambitious politician. Some people think he's a future ....
16. We'll probably meet again at some future ....

We talk about *my wife-to-be* and *my ex-husband* (not *my past husband*).

11 Phrasal verbs with *up* (CB page 133)

In the conversation in the Coursebook, Rachel says: 'I suppose I do see myself ending up there eventually.' Complete the phrases below with the verbs in the box.

bottle	cheer	look	set	turn
bring	get	put	take	

1. .... up your emotions / feelings / how you feel
2. .... you up on the sofa / for the night
3. .... up a bit / It's not that bad.
4. .... up on the doorstep / unexpectedly / out of the blue / the volume
5. .... up tennis / a lot of time / space
6. .... up a company / in business
7. .... up a word in a dictionary / the time of the train
8. .... up children / a few problems
9. .... up early in the morning / late at the weekend

Now answer these questions.

10. Do you bottle up your feelings or are you good at letting them out?
11. Have you ever put somebody up for the night?
12. When was the last time you turned up unexpectedly on someone's doorstep? Were they pleased to see you?

20 The world of work

1 Working conditions (CB pages 138, 139, 140)

Can you remember the missing words? Complete these sentences.

1. My wife's on . . . . leave at the moment.
2. I can't afford to be ill, because I don't get . . . . pay.
3. I get to travel quite a lot in my job – that's one of the . . . .
4. How much . . . . tax do you pay?
5. I just want to be . . . . the same as the full-time staff.
6. I've always had a job. I've never been . . . .
7. I'm hoping to get . . . . to deputy manager later this year.
8. I'm thinking of . . . . for a job in Paris.
9. The starting . . . . is £23,000 a year.

2 Getting a job

Put these sentences in the order that they usually happen.

a. I've started looking for a new job. . . . . .
b. I'm going for an interview. . . . . .
c. I'm getting fed up with my job. . . . . .
d. I've applied for this thing I saw in the paper. . . . . .
e. The job's going well. . . . . .
f. I've got the job. . . . . .
g. I start my new job on Monday. . . . . .
h. I've been short-listed. . . . . .

Go back and underline all the expressions with job.

Now complete the sentences below with the words and phrases in the box.

apply for	change their
found a new	give up my
lost	qualified for
train for a	

1. I've . . . . job at last! It's taken me six months.
2. I'm sorry to say Jim has . . . . his job. They're closing the Hong Kong office.

3. I think I'll . . . . my boss's job. She's leaving to have a baby.
4. I'm not sure how I feel about people who . . . . jobs every six months.
5. . . . . new job at my age? You must be joking!
6. I'm not going to . . . . job! I'm staying here till the day I retire.
7. Are you really . . . . this job at IBM, then? I didn't know.

3 Collocations: adjective + *job*

Match the sentences 1–6 to their opposites a–f.

1. It's a well-paid job.
2. It's a boring job.
3. It's a full-time job.
4. It's a permanent job.
5. It's a responsible job.
6. It's a demanding job.

a. It's an interesting job.
b. It's a temporary job.
c. It's a menial job.
d. It's a cushy job.
e. It's a badly-paid job.
f. It's a part-time job.

Now complete the sentences below with the words in the box.

| manual | professional | high-powered |

7. Being head of a large organisation like IBM is considered a very . . . . job.
8. A builder, electrician and plumber are all . . . . jobs.
9. A doctor, teacher, or lawyer are all . . . . jobs.

Jobs which have specific training (perhaps a two-year apprenticeship) before you are fully qualified, such as an electrician or plumber, are skilled jobs.

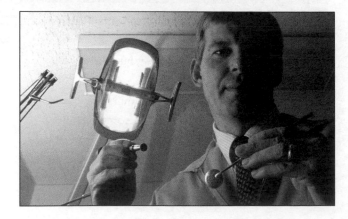

4 | Collocations: *career*

Complete the sentences below with the correct form of the verbs in the box.

change	give up	map out	ruin
embark on	hinder	pursue	sacrifice

1. She had a promising career ahead of her, but it was completely .... by her husband, who was basically jealous of her success, and persuaded her to .... it all .... and stay at home.

2. A lot of women .... their careers to start a family and allow their husbands to continue to .... theirs. I wonder if it ever happens the other way round.

3. He's very ambitious, but his career has been .... a little by a lack of opportunity. He probably needs to move on to a different company.

4. I don't really know what I want to do. I'm not one of those people who have their careers all .... in careful detail by the age of twenty-one.

5. It's much more common to .... careers today than it was for my parents' generation.

6. I did quite a few different jobs before .... a career in teaching.

5 | Expressions: *boss* or *employee*?

Who is talking: the boss to an employee, or the other way round? Write B if you think the boss is speaking or E if you think it is the employee.

1. Why are you so late? .....
2. Can I leave a bit early today? .....
3. Excellent work. Well done! .....
4. Can I arrange to see you some time today? .....
5. Can you stop what you're doing? I need to have a word with you. .....
6. Don't use the phone for personal calls. .....
7. I'd like to discuss my salary, if possible. .....
8. Sorry, it won't happen again. .....
9. Have you finished yet? .....
10. I'm doing it as fast as I can. .....

Go back and underline the useful expressions such as *Can I arrange ... .*

6 | Describing your job

Make sentences by matching the beginnings 1–8 to the endings a–h.

1. I'm stuck behind a(n) ☐
2. I spend most of my time on the ☐
3. I seem to spend most of my time in ☐
4. I often have to put in ☐
5. I have to do a lot of boring ☐
6. I spend a lot of time staring at a(n) ☐
7. I just seem to be sorting out ☐
8. I have to work to pretty tight ☐

a. quite long hours.
b. admin.
c. other people's problems all the time.
d. desk all day.
e. phone.
f. deadlines.
g. computer screen all day.
h. meetings.

7 | Two views of work!

Here are two texts about how two people in Japan earn their living. Complete the first text with the words in the box below.

charges	guess	ordinary	single
create	make	pays	way

Takashi Horito

Are you out of work? Perhaps thinking of changing your job? Why not do something a bit different from the (1) .... nine-to-five office job? Do what some people in Japan are doing – (2) .... your own.

Take Takashi Horito, for example, who has started his own business as a professional 'complimenter'. Horito (3) .... customers 150 yen (about £1) for a minute of non-stop compliments.

'You look great. I love the (4) .... you've had your hair done. Let me (5) .... – you're a fashion model, right? You must only be about twenty-two. I can't believe someone as attractive as you is still (6) ....'

These are the kinds of compliments he (7) .... to both men and women who want their egos boosted. It obviously works, as he can (8) .... £15–£20 an hour on a good day. He started his business after a frustrating period of looking for work after finishing university.

Complete the second text with the words in the box below.

avoiding	customer	fear	making
black	earns	injured	stressed

Kenji Mamoto

Another unusual way of (9) .... money was devised by Kenji Mamoto. He charges 1,000 yen a minute for customers to use him as a human punch bag.

For sixty seconds, a customer can try to hit and punch Kenji as much as they like with no (10) .... of retaliation. An ex-boxer, Kenji is an expert at (11) .... the punches. However, he does sometimes get (12) .... Some of his recent injuries include a bloody nose, (13) .... eyes and the odd broken rib. 'I tell the (14) .... to shout their name, age, and why they are so (15) ...., as loudly as possible, just before they attack me,' he said.

On a good evening, Mr Mamoto (16) .... up to £350. 'It's quite good money and it's an interesting way to experience life. I always wanted a job which involved meeting people. I want to continue for as long as I can.'

8 | Passing on messages

Pass on the messages below using reported speech. For example:

Mary's words: 'Tell them I'll be a bit late.' (say)
Mary *said she'd be a bit late.*

1. Simon's words: 'I'll phone Mike tomorrow.' (say)
   Simon ....

2. Mary's words: 'I'll fax it over straightaway.' (tell me)
   Mary ....

3. Mary's words: 'I'll be in the office all day.' (tell me)
   Mary ....

4. Mary's words: 'I'll call the office later on.' (say)
   Mary ....

5. Simon's words: 'You'll get them soon.' (say)
   Simon ....

Real English: *Give my regards to …*

If you want someone to give a greeting to someone else for you, you can say:
Give my regards to Bob/your wife/your boss.

Less formally, you can say:
Say hello to Sally/your dad/everyone.
Remember me to Sally/your dad/everyone.

9 | Future continuous (CB page 143)

The future continuous is useful before you ask someone to do something for you. For example:

A: Will you be seeing David later? I promised to get this book to him.
B: Yes, I should be.

A: Will you be passing the post office? Do you think you could drop this letter off for me?
B: Yes, no trouble.

Match the questions 1–8 to the linked questions or comments a–h.

1. Will you be driving home later? ☐
2. Will you be going to France again soon? ☐
3. Will you be using your computer all morning? ☐
4. Will you be seeing Tina after work? ☐
5. Will you be using your golf clubs this weekend? ☐
6. Will you be passing the bank on your way home? ☐
7. Will you be doing your homework later? ☐
8. Will you be going near the library while you're out? ☐

a. Because if you are, could you get me some more of that red wine?
b. It's just that I need to send an e-mail.
c. Because if you're not, is there any chance I could borrow them?
d. Because if you are, do you think you could give me a lift?
e. It's just that I've got a book to return.
f. Because if you are, is there any chance we could do it together?
g. Because if you are, could you pay in a cheque for me?
h. It's just that I've got a book to give her.

Notice these typical ways of continuing your request:

Because if you are, do you think you could … ?
Because if you are, could you … ?
Because if you are, is there any chance … ?
It's just that …

10 Reporting verbs

Cross out the verb which does not fit the pattern verb + pronoun + infinitive.

She *advised / asked / reminded / suggested / persuaded* me to come to the meeting.

Complete this sentence with the verb and its correct pattern.

She . . . . that I should come to the meeting.

Re-write these sentences in reported speech with verbs from above. For example:

If I were you, I'd do the sociology course at Edinburgh University.
He *advised me to do sociology at Edinburgh.*

1. Listen, you can't go to John's party. Liz is going to be there and it will only cause trouble if you turn up.
   She tried to . . . .

2. You won't forget to back up your files, will you?
   He . . . .

3. Will you water my plants while I'm away?
   She . . . .

11 Writing: a report

Sample report
Complete each paragraph with the words given.

Is it all about money?

aim	based on	factor	survey

The (1) . . . . of this report is to summarise the results of a(n) (2) . . . ., which was used to find out whether people consider money to be the most important (3) . . . . when choosing a job. The report is (4) . . . . a survey of fifty people.

The survey

consisted of	rank	took part in

The survey (5) . . . . asking people about five job-satisfaction criteria: money, job security, flexible working hours, perks, and career prospects. Each person that (6) . . . . the survey was asked to (7) . . . . each of the criteria on a scale of 1 to 5 (1 = not important, 5 = very important).

Results

first	respectively	surprisingly

Money came (8) . . . . with 232 points, followed, perhaps (9) . . . ., by flexible working hours with 218. Job security, career prospects, and perks were ranked third, fourth and fifth, (10) . . . ., all scoring just over 200 points.

Analysis

ahead of	fact	predictable	rated

It was no surprise that money was (11) . . . . as the most important factor in a job, but flexible working hours coming second, (12) . . . . job security and career prospects, was less (13) . . . . This may have been influenced by the (14) . . . . that some of the people interviewed had lifestyles that required a certain amount of flexibility, but others just found it an attractive working condition.

Conclusion

attractive	evidence	potential	such as

On the (15) . . . . of this survey, employers need to offer (16) . . . . employees not only a(n) (17) . . . . salary, but also flexible working hours, which allows them to continue with the lifestyle of their choice. This seems to be more important than having a secure job, career prospects, and perks, (18) . . . . a company pension or company car.

Find out if money is the most important factor in choosing a job for the students in your class. Write a report on the results. Use the same formal, impersonal style you saw in the sample report above, and use appropriate headings. If you are not able to conduct a real class survey, use your imagination to create the report.

Answer Key

Introduction

1 Words, phrases, expressions
1. interested in 2. up to our eyes in work 3. at the moment 4. too (violent) for my taste 5. getting late 6. keen on 7. in a rut 8. a bit off colour
Number 8 means *ill*.

2 What is a collocation?
1. strong tea 2. getting married 3. dry wine 4. demanding job 5. make a loss 6. a (very) deep sleep 7. taken up (a sport) 8. cancel an appointment 9. (give) a piece of advice

3 Phrasal verbs
1. getting on with 2. giving up 3. go ahead 4. dragged on 5. hurry up, running out of 6. pick (you) up

4 Grammatical terms
1. g.   2. b.   3. c.   4. a.   5. d.   6. h.   7. e.   8. f.

9. r.   10. o.   11. n.   12. q.   13. j.   14. l.   15. m.   16. i.   17. p.   18. k.

1 Talking about people

1 Present simple
1. puts on 2. stands 3. start 4. causes 5. deal with 6. has 7. work 8. go 9. get up 10. opens

2 Present simple and present continuous
1. I'm working 2. I work 3. Are you doing, I'm going 4. I'm driving 5. I'm not sleeping 6. It gives 7. I read 8. is sinking 9. we're taking 10. get, I work

3 Look, sound, smell, feel
1. looks 2. smells/looks 3. sounds 4. looks 5. sounds 6. smell 7. looks 8. feel

4 Expressions with prepositions
1. (similar) to 2. (different) from 3. (responsible) for 4. (bored) with 5. (good) at

5 Phrasal verbs with *with*
1. split up with 2. get on with 3. come up with 4. keep in touch with 5. catch up with 6. put up with

6 Keep
1. absent-minded 2. boring 3. flippant 4. irresponsible 5. accident-prone 6. rude 7. vain 8. difficult

7 Expressions with *make* and *do*
1. do 2. make 3. do 4. make 5. make 6. do 7. make 8. make 9. do 10. make 11. do 12. make 13. make 14. do 15. make 16. do 17. make 18. do 19. make 20. make 21. do 22. do

8 *Make* and *do* in context
1. a good impression 2. a decision 3. progress 4. me a favour 5. military service 6. a phone call 7. noise 8. odd jobs 9. a profit/loss 10. a suggestion 11. yourself at home 12. a few changes 13. your hair 14. a lot of business 15. a Japanese course 16. a start 17. a fortune 18. an extra year

9 Countries, nationalities and languages
1. Australian, English 2. French, French 3. Germany, German 4. Portuguese, Portuguese 5. Brazil, Portuguese 6. Austrian, German 7. Sweden, Swedish 8. Poland, Polish 9. Spain, Spanish (Catalan, if she is from Catalunia) 10. Mexican, Spanish 11. Japan, Japanese 12. Chinese, Chinese 13. Greece, Greek 14. Korea, Korean 15. Thai, Thai 16. the Netherlands, Dutch 17. Denmark, Danish 18. Turkish, Turkish

10 Describing people
1. conservative 2. generous 3. knowledgeable 4. bright 5. unreliable 6. sociable

11 Adjectives and modifiers
1. straightforward 2. witty 3. laid-back 4. tricky 5. irritating 6. predictable 7. relaxing 8. distant

12 As long as
1. e.   2. c.   3. b.   4. a.   5. d.   6. f.

13 Writing: an article
1. C.   2. D.   3. A.   4. B.   5. F.   6. H.   7. E.   8. G.

2 Friends and relatives

1 Re- verbs
1. remarry 2. resit 3. rearrange 4. rephrase 5. re-use 6. reconsider 7. re-opens 8. reread 9. retrain 10. rebuild 11. rewrite 12. readjust

2 Verb collocations
1. became 2. split up with 3. began 4. track down 5. came 6. get in touch with 7. heard 8. get 9. have

3 All I want to do is ...
1. b.   2. g.   3. a.   4. f.   5. c.   6. d.   7. h.   8. e.

4 Not as ... as ...
1. not as old as he looks 2. not as much as I was expecting 3. not as easy as it looks 4. not as far as I thought 5. not as young as I used to be 6. not as boring as the last one 7. not as good as I thought it would be 8. wasn't as much fun as I was hoping

5 The more ... , the more ...
1. sooner, sooner 2. more, more 3. faster, sooner 4. older, wiser 5. sooner, better 6. longer, less

6 Crime
1. parking ticket 2. stopped 3. court 4. speeding
5. fined 6. arrested 7. shoplifting

7 Writing: a composition
1. B. 2. C. 3. A.

3 Your interests

1 Expressions with not
1. (Not) as often as I should 2. (Not) as much as I'd like
to 3. (Not) if I can avoid it 4. (Not) as much as I used
to 5. (Not) unless I have to 6. (Not) as far as I know

2 Go and …
1. have a coffee 2. get some money 3. have a look
4. ask him 5. find a table 6. get a bottle of wine
7. call a taxi 8. get it checked 9. see the doctor

3 Frequency expressions
1. three 2. Not 3. Every 4. few 5. all 6. half 7. can
8. much, whenever

4 So (do) I, Neither (do) I
1. (so) am (I) 2. (Neither) have (I) 3. (so) is (mine)
4. (Neither) did (I) 5. (So) did (I) 6. (So) did (I)

5 Used to
1. business 2. painting 3. trouble 4. weekend
5. vegetables 6. time 7. clothes 8. gym 9. usually
10. use to 11. used to 12. use to 13. used to
14. usually 15. use to 16. used to

6 Football and tennis
1. (net) B 2 (pitch) F 3. (extra time) F
4. (double fault) T 5. (set) T 6. (goal) F
7. (score) B 8. (foul) F 9. (forehand) T
10. (penalty) F 11. (court) T 12. (tie-break) T
13. (kick-off) F 14. (backhand) T 15. (fault) T

a. kick-off b. score, set c. court d. pitch e. extra time

16. (score) B 17. (volley) T 18. (pass) F
19. (serve) T 20. (kick) F 21. (foul) F
22. (win) B 23. (shoot) F 24. (send off) F

f. serving g. scores/shoots h. sent off

7 Books and newspapers
a. **Words/expressions associated with books:**
   bestseller, blockbuster, chapter, contents page, cover,
   fiction, hardback, index, non-fiction, paperback, plot
b. **Words/expressions associated with
   newspapers:** article, daily, editorial, feature column,
   front page, headlines, horoscope, jobs page, sports
   section, tabloid, yesterday's

1. horoscope 2. sports section 3. hardback
4. non-fiction 5. index 6. chapter

8 Go, play or do?
1. go 2. play 3. go 4. does 5. does 6. goes 7. doing
8. play 9. go 10. do 11. play 12. go

9 Prepositions
1. on 2. in 3. at 4. about 5. with 6. at 7. (good) at
8. (keen) on 9. (mad) about 10. (pleased) with
11. (interested) in 12. (bad) at 13. good with
14. annoyed with 15. impressed by 16. famous for

4 Unusual interests

1 -ing forms
1. b. 2. e. 3. g. 4. c. 5. f. 6. d. 7. a.

2 Paragraph ordering
The correct order is: B, A, D, C, G, E, F

3 Otherwise
1. c. 2. a. 3. e. 4. f. 5. d. 6. b.

4 More -ing forms
1. trying 2. relaxing 3. looking after 4. talking
5. looking 6. changing 7. closing

5 Need + -ing
1. mending 2. painting 3. cleaning 4. doing
5. plugging in 6. ironing 7. signing 8. washing

6 Prepositions
1. against 2. of 3. on 4. in 5. from 6. in 7. of
8. for 9. in

7 Abbreviations
1. as soon as possible 2. for the attention of (used in
faxes, memos and letters) 3. please turn over (meaning
there is something more to read on the other side)
4. please reply (usually written on invitations, from the
French: répondez s'il vous plaît) 5. information
6. minimum 7. maximum 8. department
9. approximately 10. care of (written on an envelope
when you are writing to someone whose address is not
their own. For example: Frank Barratt, c/o Mr and Mrs
Dudley, 17 Winston Road, Derby) 11. arrive 12. depart
13. estimated time of arrival 14. for example (from the
Latin: exempli gratia) 15. to be announced (for example:
The next meeting will be at the London office, date and
time tba) 16. to be confirmed 17. for your information
18. by the way 19. used on a business letter or e-mail
to say that a copy is being sent to the person
mentioned 20. blind cc (when a person has been sent a
copy of an e-mail but without the knowledge of the
person to whom this is addressed)
21. laughs out loud (used in e-mails or text messages)

8 Collocations: decision
1. announced 2. live with 3. faced with 4. approve of
5. make 6. vindicates 7. overturned 8. putting it off

9 Words ending in -ism
1. f. 2. a. 3. d. 4. g. 5. b. 6. c. 7. h. 8. e.

10 Writing: an article
1. challenge 2. leads 3. give 4. expect 5. has 6. beats
7. meet 8. respect

5 Big decisions

1 Giving explanations: past perfect continuous
1. c. 2. f. 3. e. 4. b. 5. a. 6. d.

2 What's the job?
1. surgeon 2. mechanic 3. bouncer 4. plumber
5. vet 6. soldier 7. lawyer 8. ticket inspector
9. traffic warden 10. comedian

3 Second conditionals
1. be, could 2. could, can't 3. do, were 4. bother, were
5. do, paid 6. die, happened

4 Wish and conditionals
1. I wish I didn't have to work (this weekend).
2. I wish I could afford (to go on holiday).
3. I wish there weren't (so many tourists here).
4. I wish we had (a bigger car).
5. I wish I lived (a bit nearer the city).
6. If I had my car, I could give you a lift.
7. I'd phone him if I had his number.
8. I'd learn a foreign language if I had enough time.
9. If he spoke more clearly, people would understand what he says.
10. earned, did
11. was, had
12. spoke/knew/could speak

5 Famous conditionals
1. wolves 2. misinformed 3. borrow 4. pleasure
5. lonely

6 Question tags
1. aren't you? 2. don't you? 3. can't you? 4. isn't he?
5. do they? 6. is it? 7. isn't it? 8. doesn't it? 9. is it?
10. aren't they? 11. does she? 12. doesn't she?
13. aren't we? 14. won't we? 15. aren't I? 16. aren't I?

7 You don't … , do you?
1. a. 2. b. 3. c. 4. c. 5. b. 6. a. 7. b. 8. c.
9. b. 10. a. 11. b. 12. c.

8 I knew I'd have to …
1. c. 2. b. 3. a. 4. e. 5. f. 6. h. 7. j. 8. g.
9. i. 10. d.

9 Stuck
1. stuck in an office 2. stuck in traffic 3. it's stuck
4. get stuck 5. stuck in a rut 6. stuck with it

10 It's just as well
1. e. 2. c. 3. b. 4. a. 5. d. 6. g. 7. h. 8. j.
9. f. 10. i

11 Encouraging expressions
1. It's worth a try.
2. You've got nothing to lose.
3. You'll never know unless you try.
4. It's now or never.
5. It's a piece of cake.
6. There's only one way to find out.
7. What's the worst that could happen?

12 Collocations
1. g. 2. a. 3. h. 4. c. 5. b. 6. e. 7. d. 8. f.

13 Why? How come?
1. how come 2. how come 3. why 4. how come
5. why 6. why 7. how come 8. why

6 Flying

1 Airports and planes
1. trolley 2. check-in desk 3. delay 4. passport control
5. departure lounge 6. screens 7. boarding
8. departure gate 9. board

10. window 11. flier 12. landing 13. airline 14. hand
15. locker 16. reclaim 17. Customs

2 Idioms focus
1. corner 2. way 3. road 4. end 5. nowhere
6. turning 7. step 8. bridge 9. light

a. just around the corner
b. there's still a long way to go
c. I've reached the end of the road
d. the end is in sight
e. I'm going nowhere fast
f. there's no turning back
g. one step at a time
h. we'll cross that bridge when we come to it
i. there's light at the end of the tunnel

3 Phrasal verbs with up
1. made 2. picked 3. split 4. turned 5. come
6. freshen 7. bottle 8. set

4 Comparatives
1. more expensive 2. milder 3. easier 4. better
5. tougher 6. younger 7. more interesting 8. older

5 Absolutely
1. i. 2. d. 3. b. 4. a. 5. f. 6. g. 7. c. 8. j.
9. h. 10. e.

11. absolutely freezing 12. absolutely enormous
13. absolutely delighted 14. absolutely devastated
15. absolutely brilliant 16. absolutely fascinating
17. absolutely terrified 18. absolutely delicious
19. absolutely exhausted 20. absolutely tiny

6 Infinitive or -ing form 1
1. taking 2. to go 3. to come 4. to arrive 5. to meet
6. making 7. living, working 8. to go 9. to persuade
10. to succeed 11. driving 12. to persuade
13. doing 14. to post 15. to arrive 16. living

7 Infinitive or -ing form 2
1. travelling 2. to speak 3. going 4. to take 5. to catch
6. speaking 7. to phone 8. to spend 9. getting 10. to
have 11. playing 12. to close 13. phoning 14. to find
15. to have 16. making

8 Quick verb check
Verb + infinitive: agree, aim, arrange, deserve, fail, hope, learn, manage, offer, promise, refuse, threaten

Verb + -ing form: admit, avoid, consider, deny, fancy, finish, imagine, involve, practise, risk

9 Expressions with in
1. in common 2. in a minute 3. in a hurry 4. in time
5. in trouble 6. in particular 7. In the end 8. in general
9. in public 10. in theory, in practice

10 Expressions with *mind*
1. I changed my mind.
2. It completely slipped my mind.
3. I'll bear that in mind.
4. I haven't made up my mind.
5. Never mind.
6. Nowhere springs to mind.
7. You must be out of your mind.

11 Writing: a formal letter
1. enclosed 2. full 3. due 4. local 5. sign
6. approximately 7. regret 8. refunded. 9. prompt
10. opportunity 11. hesitate 12. further 13. sincerely

7 | Your weekend

1 Future arrangements
1. are (you) going 2, is going 3. is working 4. are (they)
having 5. is taking 6. are (you) taking 7. are (they
actually) having 8. Are (they) getting
9. are getting

2 Will/won't
1. won't, will 2. won't, will 3. will, won't 4. will, won't
5. won't, will 6. will, won't 7. won't, will 8. will, won't

3 *Going to and 'll*
1. 'll join 2. 'm going to be 3. 'll have 4. 'll show
5. 'll give 6. 're going to be 7. 'm going to phone

4 Asking about plans
1. Are you doing anything this weekend?
2. What are you up to this weekend?
3. Have you got any plans for the weekend?
4. Are you doing anything nice this weekend?
5. Have you got any holiday plans?
6. Are you planning to go away this year?
7. No. Why do you ask?
8. Oh, nothing special – how about you?
9. I haven't really decided yet.
10. No. I can't really afford it this year.

5 Collocations: *meeting, appointment, date*
1. a date 2. an appointment 3. a meeting
4. appointment 5. meeting 6. date

7. meeting 8. date 9. appointment 10. meeting
11. date 12. date 13. meeting 14. appointment

6 Reading: future forms
1. c. 2. b 3. d. 4. e. 5. a.

6. leads a team 7. starts in London 8. heads for Dover
9. continues via the Tunnel 10. face the steep climb

11. bound to 12. hopes to 13. determined to
14. expect to

7 Myself
1. f. 2. e. 3. b. 4. d. 5. a. 6. c.

8 Going to have to
1. c. 2. a. 3. b. 4. e. 5. f. 6. g. 7. h. 8. d.

8 | Party animals

1 Try and …
1. c. 2. a. 3. b. 4. e. 5. f 6. d.

2 Time prepositions: *at, on, in*
1. **It'll be ready at:** the weekend, lunchtime, Christmas, four o'clock
2. **It'll be ready on:** Monday morning, March 4th, Saturday
3. **It'll be ready in:** a few minutes, about an hour, the summer, March, 2009
4. Wednesday 16th   5. Thursday 17th
6. Monday 28th   7. Monday 21st
8. Tuesday 22nd   9. Tuesday 29th
10. Saturday 12th   11. Thursday 24th
12. Wednesday 16th   13. Wednesday 23rd

3 It's a great place
1. a 2. c 3. a 4. a. 5. a 6. b 7. c 8. b
9. b 10. c 11. a 12. b 13. c 14. b 15. b/c
16. b 17. c 18. a

4 Verb collocations
1. introducing 2. crack down on 3. proposing 4. allow
5. break up 6. make 7. getting 8. come up against
9. gave 10. tackle

5 Weak, weaken
1. c. 2. a. 3. b. 4. d.

5. shorten 6. widen 7. tighten 8. deepen

9. f. 10. g. 11. e.

12. strengthen 13. lengthen 14. loosen

6 Expressions with *give*
1. regards 2. advice 3. message 4. lift 5. answer
6. headache 7. hand 8. priority

7 Time and money
1a. spend 1b. spent 2a. run out of 2b. ran out of
3a. save 3b. save 4a. waste 4b. waste 5a. worth
5b. worth 6a. spare 6b. spare 7a. can't afford
7b. can't afford 8a. short of 8b. short of

8 Verb + preposition
1. I agree + with + b. (everything you said/you/your idea in principle)
2. It depends + on + g. (the weather/how I'm feeling/more than one thing)
3. I worry + about + f. (the future/not having enough money/my daughter)
4. I'm waiting + for + e. (a cheque to come through/them to phone me back/a fax)
5. I'm looking + for + h. (something more in life/a new job/the shoe department)
6. He insisted + on + d. (paying for himself/having everything in writing/punctuality at all times)
7. Don't blame me + for + a. (what happened/something you did/the mistake)
8. That reminds me + of + c. (something that happened last week/a holiday I had in Wales once/the time we lost our car keys)

9 Writing: a story

1. looking forward to 2. catch up with 3. call
4. missed

5. warming up/to warm up 6. sensed 7. sitting around
8. got engaged

9. spent 10. put on 11. insisted 12. died

9 Last night

1 Collocations: have, get

1. day 2. problems 3. argument 4. air 5. something to
eat 6. back 7. phone call 8. annoyed 9. home
10. shower 11. changed 12. dinner 13. attacked
14. to bed

Expressions with have: an argument, a (bad) day,
dinner, a phone call, problems, a shower, something to
eat

Expressions with get: (fresh) air, annoyed, attacked,
back, changed, home, a phone call, something to eat,
to bed

2 Had to

1. c. 2. h. 3. a. 4. f. 5. j. 6. d. 7. g. 8. b. 9. i.
10. e.

3 Managed to

1. managed to park 2. managed to get tickets
3. managed to persuade 4. managed to get 5. managed
to find 6. Did you manage to get

4 Sleep and dreams

1. b. 2. c. 3. a.

4. it went like a dream 5. It was an absolute nightmare
6. it's like a dream come true 7. Let's sleep on it

5 Responding with auxiliaries

1. Has, did 2. Did, Have 3. Have, are 4. Did, did
5. Have, did 6. Are, did 7. Are, didn't, Do 8. Did, didn't
9. could, would 10. Are, Don't 11. Were, don't, do
12. Do, do

13. trade in one car for another 14. on the way to
work 15. go out with someone you like 16. get home
in time 17. move out of town 18. bore yourself to
death

6 I bet + auxiliary

1. did 2. are 3. have 4. will 5. was 6. was 7. can't
8. do

7 Until

1. It didn't finish until half past four.
2. It didn't open until quarter past nine.
3. I didn't start driving until I was thirty-five.
4. We didn't get home until 2 am.
5. John didn't get married until he was thirty-nine.
6. My father didn't retire until he was seventy.

8 So/such

1. such (a good time) 2. such (a lot of noise) 3. such (a
pity) 4. such (a shock) 5. such (a windy day) 6. such
(bad luck) 7. so (cheap) 8. so (disappointing) 9. so (few
people) 10. such (fun) 11. so (funny)
12. so (interesting) 13. so (many people)
14. so (much money)

15. such a windy day 16. so cheap 17. so much money
18. such a shock 19. so many people, such a lot of noise

10 Relationships

1 He fancies you!

1. find 2. falls 3. fancies, flirting 4. seeing, finished with
5. ask (Rachel) out 6. chat up

2 Vocabulary: prefixes

un- : unattractive, unbearable, unimaginative
dis- : dishonest, disorganised, disrespectful
ir- : irrelevant, irresponsible
in- : informal, insane, insecure

1. unbearable 2. unattractive 3. unimaginative
4. disorganised 5. dishonest 6. disrespectful
7. irresponsible 8. irrelevant 9. insecure 10. insane
11. informal

3 Expressions with break

c. break my mind

1. break my heart 2. breaking the law 3. breaking my
concentration 4. break the habit 5. broke the silence

4 Phrasal verbs with break

1. down 2. up 3. off 4. out 5. in 6. down 7. down, up
8. out 9. into

5 Expressions with on 1

1. on strike 2. on time 3. On foot 4. on business
5. on fire 6. on holiday 7. on drugs 8. on line

6 Expressions with on 2

1. on the map 2. on the computer 3. on the first floor
4. on the other line 5. on the motorway 6. on
computer

7 Modal verb expressions

1. I could be wrong, of course.
   I must be mad, agreeing to this!
   I wouldn't be surprised.
   I couldn't agree more.
2. You can say that again.
   You should've known better.
   You might be right, but I doubt it.
   You must be joking.
3. It wouldn't surprise me.
   It shouldn't be a problem.
   It couldn't have come at a worse time.
   It might work, but I doubt it!
4. There must be a mistake.
   There shouldn't be any problem.
   There can't be any tickets left.
   There must've been thousands.

8 Won't
1. won't stop 2. won't open 3. won't apologise
4. won't (you) help 5. won't lend 6. won't grow

9 *Can't have/must have* + past participle
1. can't 2. must 3. must 4. can't 5. can't

11 Telling stories

1 Finish the story
… dropped the man while they were carrying him down the stairs!

2 Adverbs 1
1. accidentally 2. suddenly 3. instantly 4. surprisingly
5. fortunately 6. Sadly

3 Adverbs 2
1. Luckily 2. Not surprisingly 3. eventually
4. unfortunately

4 Adverbs 3
1. To begin with 2. later on 3. Suddenly 4. In the
distance 5. The next thing we knew 6. Amazingly
7. Unfortunately

5 Shall I … or not?
1. c. 2. b. 3. a.

4. h. 5. d. 6. e. 7. g. 8. f.

6 Have something done
1. pierced 2. taken 3. cut 4. installed 5. upgraded
6. redecorated 7. serviced 8. re-designed

7 *-ing* clauses
1. minding 2. waiting 3. watching 4. finishing
5. wondering 6. thinking

7. b. 8. e. 9. a. 10. c. 11. d. 12. f.

13. h. 14. j. 15. g. 16. k. 17. l. 18. i

8 Train vocabulary
1. standing 2. platform 3. calling 4. travel 5. coaches
6. change 7. buffet service

8. £14.50 9. When are you coming back? 10. So you
want a day return, that's £15.50. 11. That's an ordinary
return, that's £22.60. 12. In about five minutes.
13. Number 4.

9 Storytelling expressions
1. go on 2. Well 3. Lucky you 4. anyway 5. guess what
6. You're joking 7. to cut a long story short

10 Vocabulary
1. d. 2. c. 3. b. 4. a. 5. a. 6. d.

12 Difficult to believe

1 Cash and banks
1. b. 2. f. 3. c. 4. g. 5. e. 6. a. 7. d.

8. local currency 9. traveller's cheques 10. credit card
11. exchange rate 12. cash machine 13. PIN number
14. bank account

15. amount 16. cash 17. withdraw 18. open

2 Money expressions
1. pick up 2. ripped off 3. treated 4. splash out on
5. cost 6. tighten 7. spending 8. watch

3 I shouldn't have done that
1. should have told 2. shouldn't have told 3. should
have stayed 4. shouldn't have gone 5. should have
behaved

4 Past simple and past continuous
1. was driving 2. realised 3. needed 4. was filling up
5. went 6. finished 7. went 8. returned 9. realised
10. offered 11. drove 12. was waiting 13 told

5 Pairs of verbs
1. arrived / rolling
2. had / waiting
3. lost / shopping
4. came / leaving
5. didn't see / arguing
6. got / brushing
7. knocked / chasing
8. fell / trying

6 Conjunctions: *while, during, for*
1. while 2. for 3. during 4. while 5. during 6. for

7. just as 8. while 9. Just as 10. while 11. just as
12. while

7 *Some* and *any*
1. A 2. NA 3. N 4. NA 5. NA 6. A

7. any 8. any 9. some 10. someone, something
11. anywhere 12. somewhere

8 Expressions with *take*
1. photo 2. size 3. long 4. sugar 5. aspirins 6. time
7. taxi 8. risks 9. coat 10. advantage

9 Vague language
1. forty 2. thirty 3. four 4. two 5. four 6. one

7. anything 8. something 9. something 10. something
11. anything 12. something

13 Old friends

1 Past simple and present perfect
1. has ever seen 2. played 3. scored 4. won 5. scored
6. started 7. joined 8. has made 9. has played
10. became 11. was 12. married 13. has won
14. played 15. represented 16. signed 17. suffered
18. only played 19. won 20. ended 21. has ever seen

2 Present perfect simple and present perfect continuous
1. Have you seen 2. Have you been seeing 3. I've been trying 4. I've tried 5. I've been taking 6. It's taken
7. has been smoking 8. Have you been waiting

3 For/since
1. for 2. since 3. for 4. since 5. for 6. since 7. for
8. since 9. since 10. for

4 Expressions with *for*
1. for Christmas 2. for sale 3. for her age 4. for lunch
5. for next Monday 6. for more details

7. late for 8. famous for 9. ready for 10. sorry for
11. responsible for 12. good for

5 Ending a conversation
1. Well, I really must be going.
2. Well, it was nice talking to you.
3. Right, I'd better be going.
4. Right, it's time I was going.
5. Well, it's nice to see you again.

6 *It's time* + past simple
1. It's time I started my homework.
2. It's time you decided what you really want to do with your life.
3. It's time I learned to drive.
4. It's time I cleaned my flat.
5. It's time the government did something about old age pensions.
6. It's time I went to the dentist for a check-up.
7. It's time I had/got my bike fixed.

7 Still, yet, already
1. yet 2. already 3. still 4. still 5. yet 6. already 7. yet
8. yet, still

9. a. 10. b. 11. a. 12. a. 13. b.

14. We still haven't heard a thing from the insurance company.
15. Are you still working for IBM?
16. Are you still annoyed with me?
17. Hurry up! We've still got to get our tickets.
18. It's still raining.
19. The post still hasn't arrived.
20. In spite of all your arguments, I still think you're wrong.
21. What still needs to be done?

8 I wish
1. had listened 2. hadn't bothered 3. had spent
4. had kept in touch with 5. had realised
6. had told

14 Art

1 Expressing disapproval
1. What is that that supposed to be?
2. Are they having a laugh?
3. My five-year-old could do better than that.
4. You call that art!
5. It doesn't make any sense at all!
6. That's the most ridiculous thing I've ever seen!

2 Not recommending something
1. d. 2. a. 3. c. 4. b.

3 Collocations: *cause*
1. sensation, riot 2. damage 3. accidents 4. chaos
5. outrage

4 Adding a comment
1. b. 2. g. 3. f. 4. a. 5. d. 6. e. 7. c.

5 Believe it or not
1. A. 2. D. 3. B. 4. C.

6 Adjective + preposition
1. c. 2. a. 3. d. 4. b.

5. good at 6. relevant to 7. responsible for 8. typical of

9. typical of

10. f. 11. h. 12. e. 13. g.

14. suitable for 15. similar to 16. satisfied with
17. aware of 18. aware of 19. similar to 20. satisfied with 21. suitable for

7 The or no the
1. the 2. the 3. – 4. – 5. the 6. the 7. – 8. the 9. –

8 Remind, remember
1. reminds 2. remind 3. remind 4. remember, remind
5. reminds 6. Remember

7. reminds 8. Remember 9. remind 10. remember
11. reminds 12. remind 13. remind

14. remember 15. remembered
Another way of saying 'Remember me to your wife' is 'Say hello to your wife for me'.

9 I keep meaning to …
1. c. 2. f. 3. b. 4. d. 5. a. 6. e.

10 Writing: an article
1. B. 2. C. 3. A.

15 Describing things

1 Taste, smell, feel
It tastes: bitter, bland, delicious, disgusting, fresh, horrible, off, sharp, sour, spicy, sweet
It smells: delicious, disgusting, fresh, horrible, off, sour, spicy, sweet
It feels: cold, disgusting, fresh, hard, horrible, smooth, sharp, soft, wet

1. Silk feels smooth/soft.
2. Lemons taste bitter/delicious/horrible/sharp/sour.
3. Indian food tastes delicious/disgusting/horrible/spicy.
4. This coffee tastes bitter/bland/cold/delicious/disgusting/fresh/horrible.
5. I can smell delicious freshly-baked bread.
6. This milk smells disgusting/horrible/off/sour. Don't drink it.

2 Opposites
1. strong/mature 2. dry 3. mild 4. light 5. dark/plain
6. raw 7. fresh 8. rare 9. sparkling

3 Collocations
1. strong, strong 2. strong 3. weak 4. strong
5. weak 6. strong

7. slight 8. strong 9. firm 10. strong 11. slight
12. mild 13. slight 14. firm

Strong: accent, cheese, coffee, leader, management, possibility, pound, tea
Mild: cheese
Firm: believer, favourite
Slight: accent, headache, possibility
Weak: coffee, leader, management, pound, tea

4 Linked questions
1. b. 2. c. 3. g. 4. d. 5. f. 6. e. 7. h. 8. a.
i. 1. ii. 6. iii 4.

5 Considering, although
1. b. 2. d. 3. f. 4. c. 5. e. 6. h. 7. a. 8. g.

9. k. 10. n. 11. m. 12. l. 13. i. 14. j.

6 In spite of
1. in spite of his professional success 2. in spite of the cost 3. in spite of her parents' opposition 4. In spite of his injury 5. in spite of the snow 6. in spite of their promises

7 … , though
1. b. 2. d. 3. a. 4. c 5. f. 6. g. 7. h. 8. e.

8 Negative questions
1. Aren't you coming? 2. Didn't you get it? 3. Haven't you heard? 4. Don't you like it?

5. Didn't anyone tell you? 6. Wasn't it open? 7. Haven't you seen it? 8. Don't you remember?

9 Expressions with *way*
1. the other way round 2. either way 3. by the way
4. no way 5. change his ways 6. out of your way

10 Easily the biggest
1. c. 2. a. 3. i. 4. e. 5. j. 6. f. 7. d. 8. b.
9. g. 10. h.

11 Comparison
1. much more interesting 2. much funnier 3. much easier 4. much worse 5. much more comfortable
6. much younger

7. but not as difficult as I was expecting 8. but not as full as I was expecting 9. but not as warm as I was expecting 10. but not as many as I was expecting

12 Must've
1. gone 2. been 3. left 4. switched 5. got 6. joined

16 Films and television

1 At the cinema
1. matinee 2. rows 3. screen 4. trailers 5. subtitles
6. dubbed 7. interval 8. credits

2 Water metaphors
1. overflowing 2. trickling, flooded 3. dried up
4. pouring 5. surged

a. trickle b. dry up c. flood d. pour e. overflow
f. surge

3 -ed adjectives
1. disappointed 2. shocked 3. delighted 4. excited
5. pleased 6. annoyed

7. b. 8. a. 9. d. 10. e. 11. c. 12. f.

Hidden collocations
13. (not as good as I was) expecting 14. make (a mistake) 15. pass (your driving test) 16. (the difference) between (X and Y) 17. (arrested) for (shoplifting) 18. stuck (in a traffic jam)

4 The best film I've ever …
1. seen 2. visited 3. made 4. experienced 5. had
6. done 7. made 8. heard 9. had 10. met

5 Past perfect
1. had gone 2. wanted 3. had already tried
4. didn't work 5. advised 6. returned 7. asked
8. had counted/counted 9. had all gone

6 Prepositional phrases
1. in front of 2. next to 3. to the left 4. behind
5. on the floor 6. out of the way 7. over 8. on top of

7 Typical mistakes
1. I'm going home. See you tomorrow.
2. I'm going to Ireland next summer.
3. I live near the coast.
4. The bank's opposite the post office.
5. Go along the street and turn left.
6. Did you come by bus?
7. No, I came on foot.
8. That's typical of you!

8 Expressions with *out of*
1. out of petrol 2. out of work 3. out of my depth
4. out of your mind 5. out of the question 6. out of fashion 7. out of sight 8. out of control

9 Mixed conditionals

1. would still be living 2. would probably have 3. would probably be able to speak 4. wouldn't have missed, wouldn't be standing 5. hadn't been 6. hadn't lent 7. hadn't come into 8. hadn't spent

17 Cars and cities

1 *If* suggestions

1. It would be really great if they
2. It'd be more useful if they
3. It'd be far better if they
4. What would be really good is if they

5. c. 6. b. 7. a. 8. d.

2 Auxiliary verbs

1. I don't like swimming, but I do like going to the beach just to sunbathe.
2. It's not the best film I've ever seen, but it does get more interesting towards the end.
3. I know you're annoyed, but I do think you're over-reacting a bit.
4. It does seem pretty cheap, but then again it does have a little scratch on it.
5. I don't mind people being late when they can't help it, but I do mind when people are late and they think it doesn't matter.
6. Cambridge is a great place to live, but it does get a bit crowded in the summer.
7. The speed that cars go round here does worry me. They should do something about it.

3 Cars

1. dashboard 2. glove compartment 3. gear stick 4. clutch 5. brake 6. accelerator 7. handbrake 8. boot 9. windscreen 10. bonnet 11. aerial 12. wheel 13. wing mirror 14. tyre

4 Traffic signs

1. out 2. limit/zone 3. black 4. dual 5. of, wild 6. level

5 Traffic offences

1. speeding 2. ticket 3. light, fine 4. seatbelt 5. Drink

6 The fact that

1. What really annoys me is the fact that the government knows there's a problem, but doesn't want to do anything about it.
2. The thing that really annoys me is the fact that nobody takes us seriously.
3. You're forgetting the fact that some people don't live near a regular bus service, though.
4. The reason I don't take the bus more often is the fact that they never arrive on time.

7 Compound adjectives

1. g. 2. a. 3. b. 4. f. 5. h. 6. d. 7. e. 8. c. 9. a two-week holiday 10. an eight-hour day 11. a three-year-old boy 12. a ten-year jail sentence 13. a thirty-mile-an-hour limit 14. a two-litre engine 15. a £200-fine 16. a seven-day-a-week job

8 Make, let

1. let 2. let 3. made 4. made 5. made 6. let 7. let 8. let

9 The passive

1. has been postponed 2. haven't been invited 3. has been stolen 4. has been re-decorated 5. has definitely been sent 6. Have you been vaccinated

7. will be picked up, driven 8. will be given 9. will be flown 10. will be decided

11. included 12. served 13. cleaned 14. vacated, handed in 15. ordered 16. purchased 17. locked

There are two passives:
• 'He was given a choice.'
• 'The politician's brain has never been used.'

10 Expressions with *all*

1. We had to start all over again.
2. It's sad. He lives all by himself and no one visits him as far as I know.
3. And they kept playing loud dance music all through the night.
4. There were hundreds of bicycles all along the side of the road.
5. Oh no! I forgot all about it.
6. His new novel is all about wartime Italy.
7. I'm sorry. It's all my fault.
8. When you saw the ghost, were you all alone?

9. all of a sudden 10. all in all 11. all over the place 12. All being well

11 Agreeing expressions

1. That's exactly what I think.
2. I couldn't agree more.
3. Yes, I know what you mean.
4. Tell me about it!
5. You can say that again.
6. You took the words right out of my mouth.

12 Writing: a balanced composition

1. increasing all the time 2. results in 3. knock-on effect 4. encouraging 5. For example 6. clear-cut issue

18 Annoying things

1 Verb collocations

1. tackle 2. banned 3. delayed 4. stick 5. breaking 6. bringing 7. get 8. reinforce

2 Collocations: *issue*

1. complicating 2. avoiding 3. clarify 4. tackle

5. environmental 6. controversial 7. real 8. political

3 Phrasal verbs

1. up 2. down 3. up 4. out 5. up 6. up, out 7. down 8. out 9. up 10. out 11. down 12. up 13. out 14. up

4 Complaining

1. I wish they'd install air-conditioning.
2. I wish they'd provide more parking spaces.
3. I wish they'd update the computer system.
4. I wish someone would organise a Christmas party.
5. I wish they'd re-decorate the place.
6. I wish they'd increase the amount of training.
7. I wish they'd give us a pay rise.
8. I wish they'd get rid of him.

Glad, pleased, delighted
9. I'm glad they've installed air-conditioning.
10. I'm pleased they've provided more parking spaces.
11. I'm glad they've updated the computer system.
12. I'm delighted someone's organised a Christmas party.
13. I'm glad they've re-decorated the place.
14. I'm pleased they've increased the amount of training.
15. I'm glad they've given us a pay rise.
16. I'm delighted they've got rid of him.

5   Complaining and apologising
1. R   2. G   3. G   4. R   5. G   6. R   7. R   8. R
9. G   10. G

6   Explain, ask
1d.   2f.

7   Was/were going to
1. b.   2. a.   3. d.   4. c.   5. f.   6. e.

7. I thought you said you were going to come by train.
8. I thought you said you were going to buy a new pair of shoes.
9. I thought you said you were going to travel round the world.
10. I thought you said you were going to buy me a present.
11. I thought you said you were going to buy me a Rolex.
12. I thought you said you were going to ring me.

13a. I thought you said you were going to come at seven.

8   Jokes: complaining
1. I'm sorry, sir. I'll take it away and bring you something that is.
2. Then why aren't you laughing?
3. I just moved the potato and there it was.

9   Collocations: *problem*
1. deal with 2. underestimated 3. foresee 4. ran into/have run into

5. actual 6. minor, common 7. major

10 Writing: a letter of complaint
1. Firstly 2. secondly 3. despite 4. Needless to say
5. Finally 6. in order to 7. nor 8. immediately

19   Your future

1   Starting with *what*
1. h.   2. e.   3. a.   4. c.   5. d.   6. g.   7. f.   8. b.

2   I might try and …
1. b.   2. a.   3. f.   4. e.   5. d.   6. c.   7. g.   8. h.

a. i.   b. vii.   c. iii.   d. ii.   e. v.   f. viii.   g. vi.   h. iv.

3   Planning structures
1. I'd quite like to have a month in the sun
2. I'd quite like to apply for the manager's job
3. I'd quite like to work in the UK
4. I'd quite like to train as a nurse
5. I'd quite like to be able to play the piano

Cross out b.

6. i.   7. h.   8. f.   9. j.   10. g.

4   Sentence adverbs
a. eventually b. hopefully c. basically d. ideally
e. realistically

1. Ideally, realistically 2. hopefully 3. Basically
4. eventually

5   *if-* expressions
1. If all goes well 2. If everything goes according to plan
3. If that falls through 4. If all else fails

6   If + things
1. e.   2. c.   3. a.   4. b.   5. d.

7   Just do it!
1. I just don't understand how it happened.
2. Yes, I'm ready. I'll just get my coat.
3. If you could just sign at the bottom, please.
4. Can I just ask you something?
5. I just want to thank you for all your help.
6. Hold on, I'll just check.
7. Don't just sit there! Do something!
8. Don't worry. It's just a wasp.
9. That's just what I think myself.
10. It's just the wind.
11. Why don't you just resign?
12. I'll just check in the timetable.
13. Will your computer just switch itself off?
14. Is it too warm in here or is it just me?
15. What did you just say?

8   Present perfect for the future
1. 've finished 2. 've worked out 3. 've tried 4. 've checked 5. 've got off 6. 've passed 7. 've paid off
8. 've saved up

9   Future collocations
1. b.   2. f.   3. a.   4. c.   5. d.   6. e.

10 Collocations
1. c.   2. b.   3. a.   4. d.

5. lifetime 6. find 7. much 8. every 9. many 10c.

11. events 12. reference 13. generations 14. career
15. president 16. date

Phrasal verbs with *up*
1. bottle 2. put 3. cheer 4. turn 5. take 6. set 7. look
8. bring 9. get

I Working conditions
I. maternity 2. sick 3. perks 4. income 5. paid
6. unemployed 7. promoted 8. applying 9. salary

2 Getting a job
1–c. 2–a. 3–d. 4–b. 5–h. 6–f. 7–g. 8–e.

I. found a new 2. lost 3. apply for 4. change their
5. Train for a 6. give up my 7. qualified for

3 Collocations: adjective + *job*
I. e. 2. a. 3. f. 4. b. 5. c. 6. d.

7. high-powered 8. manual 9. professional

4 Collocations: *career*
I. ruined, give (it all) up 2. sacrifice, pursue 3. hindered
4. mapped out 5. change 6. embarking on

5 Expressions: *boss* or *employee*?
I. B   2. E   3. B   4. E   5. B 6. B   7. E   8. E   9. B
10. E

6 Describing your job
I. d.   2. e.   3. h.   4. a.   5. b.   6. g.   7. c.   8. f.

7 Two views of work!
I. ordinary 2. create 3. charges 4. way 5. guess
6. single 7. pays 8. make

9. making 10. fear 11. avoiding 12. injured 13. black
14. customer 15. stressed 16. earns

8 Passing on messages
1. Simon said (that) he would phone Mike
    tomorrow/the following day/the next day.
2. Mary told me (that) she would fax it over
    straightaway.
3. Mary told me (that) she would be in the office all
    day.
4. Mary said (that) she would call the office later on.
5. Simon said (that) you would get them soon.

9 Future continuous
I. d.   2. a.   3. b.   4. h.   5. c.   6. g.   7. f.   8. e.

10 Reporting verbs
The verb that does not fit the pattern is 'suggested'.
She *suggested* that I should come to the meeting.

1. She tried to persuade me not to go to John's party.
2. He reminded me to back up my files.
3. She asked me to water her plants while she was on
    holiday.

11 Writing: a report
I. aim 2. survey 3. factor 4. based on 5. consisted of
6. took part in 7. rank 8. first 9. surprisingly
10. respectively 11. rated 12. ahead of 13. predictable
14. fact 15. evidence 16. potential 17. attractive
18. such as